'Rarely does the character, love and care of the chef translate so well into the restaurant, food and into his books. As soon as I saw this book I started looking for a gap in my diary to get to the Basque Country. I think that shows the effect it had on me.' **Daniel Doherty**

'José Pizarro has brought us the best from San Sebastián – the prime destination of food lovers from all over the world, where the Basque nueva cocina was born and where the lively tapas bars are one of the attractions.' **Claudia Roden**

'When it comes to capturing the flavours of Spain, José does it so well, and so naturally!' **Monica Galetti**

'A must-buy book by a great spanish cook.' **James Martin**

'The area of the Basque Country is incredibly proud of its food heritage and who better to write about its fantastic recipes than the man with the knowledge, pedigree and heritage of José Pizarro.' **Tom Kerridge**

'Basque cookery is all about flavours. José is the master of the regional cuisine with flair.' **Pierre Koffmann**

'Pizarro is part of a very intimate group of chefs who have made Spanish food in this country as good as you get anywhere in Spain.' **Angela Hartnett**

'Basque cuisine is an important cultural pillar of a people with a passion for food. They have written many lines about how they understand Basque cuisine, but it's always exciting to see a great cook such as José, with his passion and wisdom, translating that passion into a universal language for everyone to enjoy.' **Andoni Luis Aduriz, Mugaritz**

'José is one of those very rare individuals whose food truly reflects him as a man. His food is honest and full of passion. It's a pleasure to call him a peer and a friend.' **Tom Sellers**

'The Basque region is the most food-obsessed part of a food-obsessed country, and who better to help us recreate its edible treasures than José Pizarro? Beautiful and unmissable for anyone who has ever delighted in a greedy stroll round San Sebastián.' **Marina O'Loughlin**

'I have long been riveted by the food of the Basque country – I cannot imagine anyone I'd rather read exploring those incredible flavours. Pizarro is the master of Spanish food.' **Thomasina Miers**

'José's Basque recipes are as close as you will get to having the master himself at your side, sharing his secrets and encouraging you to prepare and cook some of the tastiest food on earth.' **Chris Galvin**

To Mum and Dad, for teaching me the love of food, and for everything else.

Also, to Peter, for your love, patience and support. Without you, this would not have been possible.

José Pizarro

BASQUE

SPANISH RECIPES
FROM SAN SEBASTIÁN
& BEYOND

hardie grant books

MELBOURNE · LONDON

CONTENTS

FOREWORD

It always gives me the greatest pleasure to write a book introduction for a fellow chef. I love that intimate, special insight it brings with it for me to get to know first-hand everything about his cooking, his recipes, his culinary secrets – secrets that in truth are becoming fewer and fewer in a world that shows less restraint than ever. In this case, it is particularly exciting to write my foreword about a new work from that culinary conqueror, as this good man from Extremadura surely is, of the hearts and stomachs of the United Kingdom.

I speak about my good friend and excellent chef José Pizarro. It is a curious coincidence that we both came to the kitchen from other professions. I left my studies in technical architecture (much to the chagrin of my mother) to embrace the hard effort and sacrifices, but also excitement and stimuli, of a lifetime of cooking, with a timely transfer to the School of Hospitality in Madrid.

José was studying to be a dental technician. He finished his studies, but then realised that he had forsaken his vocation for gastronomy and did a year at the hotel school of Cáceres before beginning work in a restaurant from his area. Later I met him at the Mesón de Doña Filo de Julio Reoyo, where he began as he himself confessed, 'To find a new kitchen where my love of fresh ingredients, full of flavour and colour, began to be reflected in my dishes.'

Now, José is at the spearhead of the most interesting Hispanic cuisine in London. I have a healthy and unconcealed pride in the theme that he has developed in this new work, which has at its centre the Basque Country and, of course, prominently my home Donostia (San Sebastián).

Pintxos, cider, wonderful markets, not to mention the distinguished fish, are all emblematic of this area. There are stellar restaurants, but also homey food and, of course, the gastronomic societies.

José has shipped a bit of everything into his book to unveil the versatile personality of Basque cooking and its amazing influence on world cuisine.

Juan Mari Arzak, Chef, Arzak

INTRODUCTION

When I sat down with Kate, my publisher, and Holly, my agent, to talk about my new book, we decided that writing a book dedicated to one region in Spain that meant a lot to me, would be a really interesting way to go. I love the Basque Country. This book is all about the food, of course, but it's the people as well. I'm from Extremadura, a region that will always be at my heart, but I feel very much at home in the Basque Country too.

This book is not just about recipes from the Basque Country, it is about all of the wonderful ingredients you can find there, cooked in my style. It's also about my experiences there, time that I have spent eating, talking and having an incredible time.

I love to go to San Sebastián, not just to eat in the city that has more three-star Michelin restaurants than anywhere else in Europe, but to walk around the Old Town and visit street after street of glorious pintxos bars. Yes, the Basque Country has a reputation for culinary innovation and modern techniques, but its history and traditions go far back, and the celebration of these can be seen every day on the streets of San Sebastián and across the whole region.

For people from the Basque Country, food is the most important thing. It's sharing big plates of food around the table, it's celebrating happy occasions, it's a way of life. As much as I like visiting my friends in their Michelin kitchens, where I am always bowled over by their creativity, what I love is simple food, good ingredients sourced locally wherever possible, cooked with little fuss.

The recipes in *Basque* are a reflection of what I want to eat at home and the way I cook for family and friends. I want to show you not just some of the most popular and traditional dishes from the region, but also the quality and diversity of the ingredients that you can find there. The recipes have been inspired by what I've seen, what I've learnt, the people I've met and the respect they have for food. Far from being a lesson, I want you to pick up this book, feel inspired to cook from it and be really proud of what you can do.

You'll see that I've given the recipes the title of either Pintxos or At the Table. This is to give you some serving suggestions – pintxos being small tapas plates, and At the Table recipes being larger, main dishes. Use these recipes in the way that suits you best. Sometimes I just think anything goes!

José Pizarro

The Basque Country has a terrain that makes it just right for rearing animals. The green grass and rainy days in winter are the perfect combination and it means the meat is full of flavour, with those lucky animals living in the top of the hills.

Yes, fish is a big part of the diet in the region as the sea offers such a wealth of choice, but as it does get cold in the autumn and winter, meat is a very important part of many dishes.

You'll find that the Basques favour big hunks of meat that can be shared amongst many (or few sometimes), like a simple Txuletón (T-bone) in the *sidrerias* (cider houses) for example. I also like the way that the meat is used in pintxo dishes. Chicken wings in a *bodegón* (wine cellar) are heaven, and they're supposed to be messy, trust me. Then you have the complete opposite with a lovely delicate quail dish.

So versatile, yet all so delicious.

Pintxo

ROASTED CHICKEN WINGS WITH ROAST POTATOES, PARSLEY & GARLIC

Serves 6

24 chicken wings
6 garlic cloves, finely chopped
2 teaspoons pimentón
good pinch of chilli flakes
10 sprigs of oregano, leaves stripped
olive oil
750 g (1 lb 10 oz) floury potatoes,
    cut into smallish chunks
sea salt and freshly ground black
    pepper

Every time I go to the restaurant Bodegón Donostiarra I have the chicken wings. But I have to say that the last time I went, they were better than ever. Maybe it was because I was sitting outside on the terrace on a gorgeous July day with a really cold beer …

I once cooked chicken wings on the TV show *Saturday Kitchen*, then tried to get some later that day to cook for friends, and they were impossible to find. It seems that many more people were asking for chicken wings than normal. Maybe they saw me cook them and just had to have them! You will feel the same once you've tried this recipe.

Put the chicken wings in a dish. Mix half of the chopped garlic cloves with the pimentón, chilli flakes, half the oregano and a good glug of olive oil. Spread all over the wings and leave to marinate for at least 12 hours.

Preheat the oven to 200°C (400°F/Gas 6).

Put the potatoes into a pan of cold salted water, bring to the boil and simmer for a couple of minutes. Drain, return to the pan over a low heat and toss to fluff up the edges.

Heat a good glug of oil in a roasting tin in the oven, then toss in the potatoes. Put the chicken wings on top and roast for 45–50 minutes until it is all crispy and golden. Season with lots of salt and pepper and add the rest of the garlic and oregano.

Pintxo

HOME-CURED DUCK HAM WITH POMEGRANATE SALAD

Serves 8

4 duck breasts
200 g (7 oz) caster (superfine) sugar
300 g (10½ oz) flaky sea salt
1 tablespoon freshly ground black
    pepper

for the salad
few large handfuls of watercress
seeds of 1 pomegranate
1 tablespoon Moscatel vinegar or
    sherry vinegar
sea salt and freshly ground black
    pepper
2–3 tablespoons extra-virgin olive oil
50 g (2 oz) toasted flaked almonds

You will need to plan a little here as it will take several days for the duck to cure, but you'll feel very proud of yourself once you've done it. It took me a long time to perfect this recipe, but I'm really happy that I persevered – the end result is delicious, and it allows you to use the last of the watercress alongside the first pomegranates of the season.

Put the duck into a plastic container. Mix the sugar, salt and pepper together and cover the duck breasts with the mixture. Cover and chill in the fridge for 12 hours.

Remove the duck breasts from the curing mix and wipe with a cloth. Take a skewer and push it through one end of the duck breasts so they hang down. Tie some string around each end of the skewer, hang inside the fridge and leave to dry for 7–10 days. The meat should be firm to the touch when you squeeze it gently.

Once the duck is ready, put the watercress and pomegranate seeds in a bowl. Mix the vinegar with some seasoning and olive oil and toss with the leaves. Scatter in the almonds.

Divide the watercress and pomegranate salad between small plates. Use a very sharp knife to finely slice the cured duck and serve on top of the salad.

PORK TROTTERS, APPLE & HAZELNUT TERRINE

Serves 6

3–4 pork trotters (about
  1.8–2 kg/4–4½ lb)
2 onions, chopped
2 carrots, chopped
1 teaspoon black peppercorns
2 bay leaves
50 g (2 oz) hazelnuts
25 g (1 oz) unsalted butter
2 small dessert apples, peeled and
  chopped into small pieces
70 g (2½ oz) dried apricots, chopped
few sage leaves, finely chopped
small bunch of chives, snipped
sea salt and freshly ground black
  pepper
olive oil

I know it might be a funny thing to say, but I'm a gelatine lover, so this recipe is heaven for me. My mum always used to cook trotters in a very simple way – just boiled, deboned and then served with some onions and a garlic sauce. I actually like them prepared even more simply, just with some butter.

This recipe is the one that very often features on our menu at Pizarro and it is very popular; we normally serve it with a strawberry salad with Moscatel vinegar dressing, which really helps to cleanse the palate. This terrine will easily keep for a week in the fridge (if you can stop yourself from eating it all, that is).

Put the trotters into a pan with the onions, carrots, peppercorns and bay leaves. Cover with cold water and bring to the boil, then reduce to a simmer and cook for 3–4 hours or until the trotters are very, very tender. Remove the trotters (discard the cooking liquid) and when cool enough to handle, pull the meat and skin off the bones and roughly chop, discarding the bones.

Toast the hazelnuts in a pan until lightly golden, then tip onto a baking sheet lined with non-stick silicone or baking paper to cool before chopping roughly.

Melt the butter in a pan and gently cook the apples for a couple of minutes until starting to become tender. Add the hazelnuts, apricots and herbs, season well and cook for a few minutes more.

Add the apple mixture to the trotter meat and skin and mix well. Check the seasoning.

Line a long 450 g (1 lb) terrine or loaf tin with cling film (plastic wrap), then spoon in the mixture and fold the cling film over the top. You want to weigh the meat down to press it as it chills. Cut a piece of cardboard the same size as the top of the terrine or loaf tin, then stand heavy weights or tins of beans on top. Chill overnight.

When ready to serve, heat a pan with a little oil over a high heat. Turn out the terrine, unwrap and cut into thick slices. Sear in the pan for a few minutes each side, then serve with a green leaf salad.

Pintxo

GRIDDLED MARINATED QUAIL WITH PICKLED SHALLOTS

Serves 6

6 quail, spatchcocked
juice of 2 lemons
1 banana shallot (echalion), finely
   chopped
2 garlic cloves, finely chopped
4–5 sprigs of thyme
olive oil

for the shallots

75 ml (2½ fl oz) cider vinegar
75 ml (2½ fl oz) raspberry vinegar
50 g (2 oz) caster (superfine) sugar
6 black peppercorns
4 banana shallots (echalions), finely
   sliced
sea salt and freshly ground black
   pepper
extra-virgin olive oil

If you go to A Fuego Negro, a pintxo place in San Sebastián, something you mustn't miss is *pajarito frito* (little fried bird) – it's just amazing. I love the complexity of this dish – they marinate the bird with vermouth, roasted garlic and honey, then leave it for 24 hours so the flavours really infuse into the meat.

Here we marinate quail for the same amount of time but with lemon, garlic and thyme instead. I've kept the same pickled shallot garnish as it's a perfect combination. Happy days.

Put the quail into a dish. Mix the lemon juice with the shallot, garlic, thyme and a good amount of olive oil. Pour the mixture over the quail and marinate overnight.

The next day heat the vinegars with the caster sugar and peppercorns until the sugar has dissolved. Pour the hot vinegar over the shallots and set aside.

Heat a barbecue or chargrill pan. Once the pan is hot, remove the quail from the marinade and griddle for 15 minutes, turning, until cooked. Set aside to rest.

Drain the shallots from the vinegar, season with a little salt and pepper and add some extra-virgin olive oil. Serve with the griddled quail.

Pintxo

PIQUILLO PEPPERS STUFFED WITH OXTAIL

Serves 4–6

1.5 kg (3 lb 5 oz) oxtail
1 bottle of Txakoli or other crisp dry white wine
1 onion, finely chopped
1 carrot, finely chopped
1 celery stalk, finely chopped
1 bay leaf
5 black peppercorns
handful of parsley sprigs
olive oil
sea salt and freshly ground black pepper
750 ml (25 fl oz) fresh beef or chicken stock
2 × 220 g (8 oz) jars of piquillo peppers, drained
4 tablespoons plain (all-purpose) flour
2 free-range eggs, beaten

You will usually find piquillo peppers stuffed with cod *brandada* and sometimes with *pisto* (vegetable stew), but I think they go beautifully with rich, meaty oxtail. Oxtail is often cooked with red wine, maybe because people think the strong flavour of the oxtail will stand up to a big red. I'm turning this on its head a little, though, and using Txakoli instead. The flavour is more delicate and doesn't overpower the delicious meat.

Put the oxtail into a dish, pour over the wine and add the vegetables, bay leaf, peppercorns and parsley and marinate overnight.

Drain the oxtail and vegetables, reserving the wine, and pat dry. Heat some oil in a heavy-based pan. Season the oxtail and fry until golden on both sides, then tip into a casserole dish. Add the vegetables to the pan with a little more oil if needed and fry for 10 minutes to soften. Tip into the casserole dish. Return the wine and aromatics to the meat and add enough stock to cover.

Bring to the boil, cover, reduce to a simmer and cook for 2½–3 hours. Remove the lid for the last half an hour of cooking and reduce until the sauce thickens and the meat falls off the bones.

Remove the meat and vegetables with a slotted spoon and continue to reduce the sauce until glossy and thick. Shred the meat from the bones, mix with the vegetables and just enough sauce to coat. Keep the rest of the sauce to serve.

Stuff the peppers with the oxtail ragu. Heat a layer of oil in a pan. Dip each pepper in the flour, then in the egg, and fry for a few minutes each side until golden. Heat the rest of the sauce in a small pan. Serve the fried peppers with the sauce spooned over the top.

At the table

SALAD OF PARTRIDGE ESCABECHE, WALNUTS & FIGS

Serves 4

olive oil
2 whole partridges or 4 partridge
    breasts
sea salt and freshly ground black
    pepper
1 onion, finely chopped
1 carrot, finely chopped
2 celery stalks, finely chopped
2 garlic cloves, finely sliced
5–6 sprigs of thyme
1 fresh bay leaf
150 ml (5 fl oz) sherry vinegar
250 ml (8½ fl oz) white wine
100 g (3½ oz) walnut halves
1 frisée lettuce, washed and leaves
    separated
6 ripe figs, quartered
extra-virgin olive oil to drizzle

You'll find walnuts all over the Basque Country, they are so good. The first time I saw one, it really surprised me as they are a lot smaller than the ones we are used to in Extremadura.

I love the combination of the really fresh walnuts and fresh figs, but if you can't get fresh figs, dry ones will work very well too.

Escabeche is a way of cooking using vinegar to give a lovely flavour. It also preserves the ingredients a little so they keep longer. If you can, cook the partridge two days before and keep it in the fridge – the bird will take on more flavour from the escabeche.

Heat some olive oil in a large casserole dish. Season the partridge and brown all over, then set aside. Add the vegetables to the pan and cook for 10 minutes until tender, then add the garlic and herbs. Return the partridge to the pan and splash in the vinegar. Bubble for a minute before adding the wine. Cover and cook gently for 45 minutes until the partridge is really tender.

If the sauce is still very juicy, take the partridge out to rest and bubble the sauce away until it just coats the vegetables.

Toast the walnuts in a pan until lightly golden, then tip onto a baking sheet lined with non-stick silicone or baking paper.

Once the partridge has rested for at least 10 minutes, carve and shred the meat and toss with the vegetables and frisée lettuce. Pile onto plates and top with a few walnuts and fig quarters. Drizzle with extra-virgin olive oil and serve.

Pintxo

DUCK LIVERS.
& CHANTERELLES

Serves 4

olive oil
400 g (14 oz) duck livers, cleaned
sea salt and freshly ground black
    pepper
4 sage leaves, finely sliced
2 garlic cloves, finely sliced
2 tablespoons sherry vinegar
good knob of unsalted butter
400 g (14 oz) chanterelles
Idiazábal or manchego cheese
    shavings to serve
extra-virgin olive oil to drizzle

Walk around the market when mushrooms are in season and you will find amazing piles of chanterelles next to the most incredible ceps, it's a lovely sight. The market at Ordizia dates back to the 14th century and was the meeting point for the local producers. Nowadays, the same is still true and it's also where the prices of produce in the whole area are determined.

At the Ganbara restaurant, they serve a stunning dish using the ceps and some foie gras – this is my more down-to-earth version, which I think is just as incredible.

Heat a little oil over a high heat in a non-stick pan. Season the livers and add to the pan. Sear on one side, then turn over and add the sage and garlic and fry for a minute more. Splash in the vinegar, then remove the just-cooked livers from the pan and set aside to rest. They should still be pink in the middle.

Put the butter in the pan with the garlic and sage, add the mushrooms and fry until they are tender and coated in the juices. Season and serve with the duck livers, scattered with shavings of cheese and a drizzle of extra-virgin olive oil.

Pintxo

MARINATED WHITE ANCHOVIES, WITH TOMATOES & JAMÓN SALAD

Serves 4

500 g (1 lb 2 oz) ripe vine tomatoes, cut into wedges
1 garlic clove, finely chopped
2 teaspoons Moscatel vinegar or sherry vinegar
extra-virgin olive oil to drizzle
sea salt and freshly ground black pepper
12 boquerones
4 slices of jamón, torn into pieces

It is very popular to have tomatoes and salted anchovies together, but one day when I was cooking for friends I didn't have any salted ones so I used *boquerones* (anchovies cured in vinegar and stored in olive oil, like the ones in the picture, opposite) instead and then added some jamón. The combination of these flavours works so well – a happy accident you might say!

We are including this in the meat section as it's the jamón that really brings all of the other flavours together.

Mix the tomatoes with the garlic, vinegar and plenty of extra-virgin olive oil. Season with sea salt and plenty of black pepper.

Arrange the tomatoes on a serving plate, top with the anchovies and jamón and serve.

At the table

RABBIT WITH WHITE BEANS & CHORIZO

Serves 6

500 g (1 lb 2 oz) dried judion beans
(or dried butter beans)
olive oil
2 rabbits, jointed (ask your butcher)
sea salt and freshly ground black
pepper
200 g (7 oz) baby cooking chorizo
1 onion, finely chopped
1 carrot, finely chopped
1 celery stalk, finely chopped
3 garlic cloves, finely sliced
2 bay leaves
4–5 juniper berries, lightly crushed
500 ml (17 fl oz) dry cider
750 ml (25 fl oz) fresh, light chicken
stock

On our way back from meeting Kepa, the cheese producer, we met the most amazing family: Marcial, Matias, Mari Angeles and Marisol. They are retired and now spend their time growing and looking after vegetables.

They were not very happy with the local rabbits, which were causing them big problems in the vegetable garden.

I love to eat rabbit and I will pass this recipe onto them as it's a very good way to make use of their plentiful supply!

Soak the beans in cold water overnight. Drain and put into a pan of clean cold water. Bring to the boil and simmer for 1 hour.

Meanwhile, heat some oil in a frying pan. Season the rabbit pieces and fry all over until golden. Transfer to a casserole dish. Add the chorizo to the frying pan and cook for a few minutes until golden all over. Tip into the casserole with the rabbit.

Add the vegetables to the pan with the chorizo oil and fry for 10 minutes until softened. Add the garlic for the last minute. Scoop out with a slotted spoon (discard the rest of the oil) and add to the casserole dish.

Add the bay leaves, juniper berries and cider to the casserole, bring to the boil and simmer for 5 minutes, then add the stock. Cover and bring to the boil, then reduce to a simmer and cook for 2–2½ hours. Drain the almost cooked beans and add to the casserole for the last half an hour of cooking. Check the seasoning and serve with crusty bread to mop up the delicious juices.

At the table

T-BONE WITH ANCHOVY SALSA

Serves 4

1 large T-bone steak or 2 smaller ones
olive oil
sea salt and freshly ground black
    pepper

for the salsa
1 French shallot, finely chopped
2 garlic cloves, finely chopped
300 g (10½ oz) cherry tomatoes,
    chopped
6 salted anchovies
zest of 1 lemon
large handful of flat-leaf parsley,
    chopped
few sprigs of marjoram, leaves
    stripped
extra-virgin olive oil

One of my favourite places in San Sebastián, and it's not for the pintxos, is Bar Nestor in the old part of the town. They sell only three things – padrón peppers, tomato salad and Txuletón steak.

Be prepared to wait for your table as it is very popular and has a long history, having opened in 1980.

Some people say that you don't need a salsa or sauce if you have really good quality meat, but you must try this – I think it goes perfectly with meat, fish or vegetables, so it's a great one to master.

Preheat the oven to 200°C (400°F/Gas 6).

Heat a chargrill pan over a high heat. Rub the T-bone with oil and season well, then sear on the chargrill for a few minutes each side until it takes on lots of colour. Transfer to the oven and cook for 12–15 minutes until nicely rare in the centre. Set aside to rest for at least 10 minutes.

Meanwhile, heat a good amount of oil (about 75 ml/2½ fl oz) in a pan and gently fry the shallot for a few minutes. Add the garlic, cherry tomatoes, anchovies and lemon zest and cook slowly until the anchovies have broken down and the tomatoes are starting to become tender but not too soft. Add the parsley, marjoram and a splash of extra-virgin olive oil and spoon into a bowl.

Carve the beautiful rare T-bone and serve with the warm anchovy salsa. You can also serve with some sautéed potatoes.

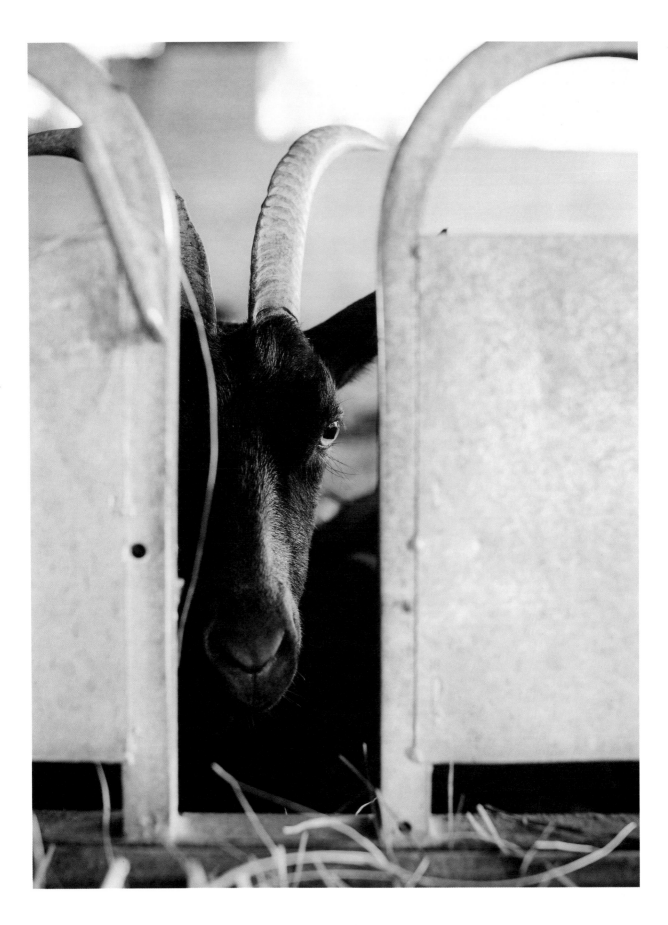

At the table

VEAL CHOPS WITH BLACK-EYED PEAS STEW

Serves 4

350 g (12 oz) dried black-eyed peas
1 onion, chopped
1 carrot, chopped
2 garlic cloves, bashed
2 bay leaves
750 ml (25 fl oz) fresh vegetable
    stock
4 veal chops
sea salt and freshly ground black
    pepper
olive oil
handful of chopped parsley

Beef is without doubt the most popular meat in the Basque Country, but veal is used widely too. I love veal – it's so tender and versatile for cooking.

I will never understand why black-eyed peas are not as popular in the UK as other beans – I think they have lots more flavour. Just cook them with a few vegetables and you will have a dish you can serve either on its own or as a side dish to go with grilled pork or any oily fish such as grilled mackerel.

Soak the peas for 12 hours in cold water, changing the water a couple of times. The next day, drain the peas and put into a pan with the onion, carrot, garlic, bay leaves and stock. Bring to the boil, then reduce to a simmer and cook for 1½–2 hours until tender and the sauce is clinging to the peas.

When the peas are cooked, season the veal chops and rub with oil. Heat a chargrill pan or heavy-based frying pan over a high heat and cook the veal for 2–3 minutes each side until cooked but still a little pink in the middle. Set aside to rest for 5–8 minutes.

Stir the parsley into the peas and serve with the veal chops.

At the table

TOMATO SOUP WITH JAMÓN & IDIAZÁBAL

Serves 6

2 kg (4½ lb) beautiful vine-ripened tomatoes
1 bulb garlic, cloves separated
olive oil
sea salt and freshly ground black pepper
1 banana shallot (echalion), finely chopped
handful of thyme sprigs, plus a few extra to garnish
1 litre (34 fl oz) fresh ham or fresh chicken stock
6 slices of baguette
6 slices of jamón
Idiazábal or manchego cheese shavings
extra-virgin olive oil to drizzle

This is my interpretation of the tomato soup that I always order at restaurant La Cuchara de San Telmo. It's a cold soup with jamón and Idiazábal. I'd never dare ask them for the recipe, but I think I've got pretty close here so I'm happy with that.

My mum always fries the tomatoes with some onion and garlic, until really well reduced, and then adds some water. This is a great way to make the soup, and I risk life and limb to say this ... but I do think that roasting the tomatoes and the garlic gives it a completely different dimension. Sorry, Mum!

Preheat the oven to 160°C (320°F/Gas 3).

Halve the tomatoes and place on two large baking sheets with the garlic. Drizzle with lots of olive oil and season well, and place in the oven, rotating the trays halfway through cooking. Roast for 45–60 minutes until slightly caramelised.

Heat a little more oil in a deep pan and gently fry the shallot for 10 minutes. Tip in the roasted tomatoes and squeeze the soft garlic from their skins and add to the pan. Throw in the thyme and pour over the stock. Bring to the boil, then simmer for 10 minutes.

Meanwhile, heat some oil in a frying pan and fry the baguette slices until golden and crisp, then break into pieces.

Spoon the soup into warmed bowls. Top with a scattering of fried baguette, the jamón slices and some cheese. Drizzle with extra-virgin olive oil, garnish with a sprig of thyme and serve.

SUKALKI – A TYPICAL BEEF RAGU

Serves 6–8

olive oil
1.5 kg (3 lb 5 oz) beef shin, cut into
    large pieces
sea salt and freshly ground black
    pepper
1 onion, finely chopped
1 carrot, finely chopped
150 ml (5 fl oz) Cognac
2 dried choricero peppers, seeds
    removed, or 2 teaspoons sweet
    pimentón
750 ml (25 fl oz) fresh beef stock
500 g (1 lb 2 oz) medium waxy
    potatoes, thickly sliced
200 g (7 oz) fresh peas

Sukalki is another traditional dish from the Basque Country, and means 'make at home' or 'stew'. It's very similar to a ragu and is traditionally found in the *sociedades* or *txoko* (traditional Basque gastronomic societies). The king of the *concursos gastronómicos* (the most popular culinary competition) takes place in Mungin and is called *Sukalki Eguna*. It's been running for decades and quite often hosts more than 300 contestants.

Heat a layer of oil in a heavy-based pan. Season the beef and fry in batches to brown all over. Transfer to a casserole dish.

Heat a little more oil and fry the onion and carrot for 10 minutes, then pour in the Cognac and carefully light it so that it flambés. Once the flames have died down, tip into the casserole with the meat. Add the dried peppers.

Add the stock and bring to the boil. Cover, reduce to a gentle simmer and cook for 3–3½ hours. Add the potatoes for the last 20–30 minutes. Once the potatoes are tender and the beef falls apart when you prod it, add the peas and cook through.

CHICKEN STEWED IN CIDER & APPLES

Serves 6

olive oil
1 free-range chicken (1.8–2 kg/4 lb–4½ lb)
sea salt and freshly ground black pepper
1 apple, peeled, cored and halved
2 onions, finely sliced
2 bay leaves
6 sage leaves
1 cinnamon stick
500 ml (17 fl oz) cider
400 ml (13 fl oz) fresh chicken stock
25 g (1 oz) unsalted butter
3 apples, peeled, cored and sliced into 8 pieces
1 teaspoon caster (superfine) sugar
75 g (2½ oz) sultanas

The Basque Country is feted across Spain, and indeed the world, for its culinary creativity. It has more three Michelin-starred restaurants than anywhere else, and I can understand why – there are so many local products that you can be inspired by here.

My inspiration for this dish, as with many of my recipes, came from seeing the ingredients together. When I see them, I just have to create a plate of food. When we were in Astarbe in a beautiful cider house, I saw the chickens hopping around the apple trees, and that was it!

Preheat the oven to 160°C (320°F/Gas 3).

Heat a layer of oil in a large casserole dish. Season the chicken inside and out and brown all over in the casserole dish. Set aside and put the halved apple inside the cavity.

Add the onions to the casserole and fry for 10 minutes to soften. Return the chicken to the pan and add the herbs and cinnamon.

Pour in the cider and bubble for a few minutes, then add the stock. Bring to the boil, then cover and transfer to the oven to cook for 1 hour.

Meanwhile, heat a little oil and the butter and fry the rest of the apples with the sugar until golden and caramelised. Add the sultanas and toss in the buttery juices. Add to the casserole about halfway through the cooking time.

Remove the lid of the casserole and turn up the oven to 220°C (430°F/Gas 7). Cook for 10 minutes more to brown the top of the chicken, then serve.

At the table

SLOW-ROASTED SHOULDER OF BABY GOAT WITH GREEN SALAD

Serves 6

2–2.5 kg (4½–5½ lb) shoulder of goat or lamb
sea salt and freshly ground black pepper
olive oil
2 glasses (250 ml/4 fl oz) of white wine
1 bay leaf
1 bulb garlic, halved around the middle
3 baby gem lettuces
2 handfuls of watercress (about 50 g/2 oz)
juice of ½ lemon
pinch of sugar
4–5 tablespoons extra-virgin olive oil
handful of chives, snipped

Goat from the Basque Region is just gorgeous; this is because the animals graze on lots of grass, producing sweet milk as well as really tasty meat. It's so delicate and tender, it's something you'll remember forever if you ever get to try it. Goat meat is becoming really popular in the UK — we almost always have it our restaurant menus, and it's a big seller.

Heat the oven to 170°C (340°F/Gas 3).

Heat a large pan over a high heat. Season the goat shoulders and rub all over with plenty of olive oil. Brown the shoulders in the pan, then transfer to a roasting tin. Pour over the wine and add the bay leaf and the garlic.

Cover with foil and roast for 2 hours, then remove the foil, turn up the oven to 200°C (400°F/Gas 6) and cook for a further 20–30 minutes to brown all over. Leave to rest.

Toss the leaves of the baby gem with the watercress. Mix the lemon juice with salt, pepper and the pinch of sugar, then drizzle in the olive oil and whisk together. Pour over the salad, scatter with the chives and toss together.

Serve the slow-roasted goat and its juices with the green salad.

At the table

BEEF CHEEKS IN RED WINE SAUCE WITH CAULIFLOWER PURÉE

Serves 4–6

for the beef cheeks
1 kg (2 lb 3 oz) beef cheeks, cut into
    large chunks
1 bottle of Rioja
2 carrots, chopped
1 onion, chopped
1 celery stalk, chopped
1 bay leaf
few sprigs of thyme
3 garlic cloves, peeled
10 black peppercorns
olive oil
sea salt and freshly ground black
    pepper
200 ml (7 fl oz) fresh beef stock

for the cauliflower purée
1 cauliflower, broken into florets
500 ml (17 fl oz) full-fat (whole) milk
50 g (2 oz) unsalted butter
sea salt and white pepper

Generally people think that beef cheeks are a winter dish, but I have to say, I love them all year round. This is an easy recipe, but it takes a little time as you need to marinate the cheeks overnight. It's really worth it though, to get those deep, earthy flavours.

I strongly suggest that you use a good-quality wine as it makes such a difference to the flavour. For extra bite and texture, I sometimes like to add some toasted flaked almonds on top, to finish it off.

Marinate the beef with all the ingredients except for the oil, seasoning and stock, ande chill in the fridge overnight. The next day, drain the beef and vegetables, reserving the wine, and set aside.

Heat a good layer of oil in a large pan, season the beef with salt and black pepper and fry in batches until browned all over. Transfer to a casserole dish. Discard most of the oil from the pan, then add in the vegetables and fry for 15 minutes until quite tender. Tip into the casserole dish with the beef. Pour in the reserved wine and top up with enough stock to cover.

Put the lid on, bring to the boil, then reduce to a simmer and cook for 2½–3 hours until really tender and falling apart.

Meanwhile cook the cauliflower. Put the florets into a pan and cover with the milk. Bring to a simmer and cook for 15 minutes until tender. Drain, reserving the milk. Use a hand blender and whiz with 50–100 ml (2–3½ fl oz) of the reserved milk and the butter until smooth and glossy. Season with salt and white pepper. Serve the beef on a good dollop of cauliflower purée, and top with some of the red wine sauce.

At the table

LAMB SHANK WITH JERUSALEM ARTICHOKES & BLACK OLIVES

Serves 6

6 lamb shanks (about 350 g/12 oz each)
sea salt and freshly ground black pepper
olive oil
750 ml–1 litre (25–34 fl oz) fresh chicken stock
600 g (1 lb 5 oz) Jerusalem artichokes, scrubbed and cut into evenly sized pieces
150 g (5 oz) pitted black olives
creamy mashed potatoes to serve
handful of chopped mint

Latxa and Carrazana are the sheep breeds from the Basque Country – they produce meat with a really sweet and delicate flavour. I always think it's amazing to see these animals walking around in the Basque countryside. Watching them always makes me hungry!

Season the lamb shanks. Heat a little oil in a casserole dish and brown the lamb shanks all over. Pour in the stock and bring to the boil. Add the artichokes and reduce to a simmer.

Cover and cook for 2–2½ hours until the lamb is falling from the bone. Stir in the olives for the last 20 minutes of cooking.

Serve with creamy mashed potatoes, scattered with fresh mint.

At the table
SUCKLING PIG

Serves 8

1 suckling pig (about 4.5 kg/9¾ lb)
2 lemons, halved
2 oranges, halved
400 ml (13 fl oz/1¾ cups) white wine
2 bay leaves
10 black peppercorns
4 cloves
75 ml (2½ fl oz/¼ cup) olive oil
75 g (2½ oz) lard
sea salt and freshly ground black
    pepper

If you have already read some of this book, you will know that La Cuchara de San Telmo is one of my favourites restaurants in San Sebastián, and their suckling pig is one dish you must try. The skin is really golden and crispy, and the meat will melt in your mouth!

If you don't have a large 'range' type oven your kitchen at home, it might be difficult to roast the whole animal. I usually cut the pig in half, through the middle of the belly, and roast the meat in two tins. Any good butcher will cut the pig for you.

Ask your butcher to clean the suckling pig and to cut it into two roughly equal-sized pieces. Make sure the pig is cleaned inside very well, leaving it with no traces of blood.

Place the suckling pig in a container, squeeze over the lemons and oranges and add the halves. Add all the other ingredients except the oil and lard. Pour 300 ml (10 fl oz/1¼ cups) water to cover. Leave in a cool place to marinate overnight.

The next day, preheat the oven to 180°C (350°F/Gas 4). Drain the suckling pig and pat dry. Score the skin with a sharp knife, then rub all over with half the oil and lard and season really well. Place the pig on its belly in a large roasting tin and roast for 20 minutes. It can be difficult to get the head end standing on its belly, so you can also cook it for half the time on one side and the other half on the other.

After 20 minutes, rub again with more oil and lard and cover the ears and tail with foil. Reduce the oven temperature to 150°C (300°F/Gas 2) and cook for 2 hours, basting with some of the liquid every 15 minutes and turning the pig if needed.

Turn the oven up to 200°C (400°F/Gas 6). Remove the foil from the ears and tail and roast the pig for a further 20 minutes or until golden and crispy. Rest for 20 minutes before serving.

At the table

ROASTED LEG OF DUCK WITH SAUTÉED CABBAGE, RAISINS & POMEGRANATE

The spring water from the Basque area is what makes the vegetables from this part of the world so special.

In this recipe, I cook the cabbage the way my mum does, for a very long time. The addition of vinegar will help to cut through the fat from the duck.

Serves 4

4 duck legs
sea salt and freshly ground black
    pepper
olive oil
2 small onions, sliced
1 star anise
pared zest of 1 orange
175 ml (6 fl oz) white wine
1 January King cabbage (or savoy)
    (about 300 g/10½ oz), finely
    shredded
150 g (5 oz) pancetta cubes
2 tablespoons Moscatel vinegar
    or sherry vinegar
handful of raisins
seeds of 1 pomegranate

Preheat the over to 150°C (300°F/Gas 2).

Season the duck legs. Heat a little oil in a pan and brown the duck legs all over. Put into a roasting tin with the onion, star anise, orange zest and wine. Cover with foil and roast for 1 hour, then remove the foil and roast for a further 30–45 minutes. Turn the heat up to 200°C (400°F/Gas 6) for a final 10 minutes to help crisp the skin.

Meanwhile, heat a little oil in a pan and add the cabbage and a splash of water. Cover and cook for 15 minutes, then remove the lid and cook for a further 5–10 minutes.

Fry the pancetta in another pan with a little oil and, when crisp, add the vinegar and deglaze the pan. Toss the pancetta through the cabbage with the raisins and pomegranate seeds. Season and serve with the roasted duck and its juices.

At the table

PORK CHOPS A LA PLANCHA WITH WHITE BEAN PURÉE & PIPERRADA

Serves 4

olive oil
2 large onions, finely sliced
2 green peppers, deseeded and
　sliced
3 Espelette peppers (or 3 Romano
　peppers and 2 teaspoons
　pimentón), sliced
sea salt and freshly ground black
　pepper
2 sprigs of rosemary
2 garlic cloves, squashed with
　a knife
4 pork chops
500 g (1 lb 2 oz) jar of white beans,
　drained and rinsed
extra-virgin olive oil to drizzle

There's not much that can compare with a juicy pork chop and if you get to eat some *Baserriko Txerria* pork, you will be in heaven. Piperrada is a sauce made with onions, green peppers and the local pepper called *Espelette,* which is cultivated in cooler areas of the region. Once collected, *Espelette* has many uses and you will often find it in jars or as a paste.

Heat a little oil in a pan and gently fry the onions and all the peppers together with some salt and pepper until slightly softened, then set aside.

Heat a good amount of oil in a heavy-based non-stick pan and very gently infuse with the rosemary and garlic for a few minutes. Remove the aromatics and set aside half the oil for later.

Season the pork chops and fry in the remaining infused oil over a high heat for 2–3 minutes each side. Remove from the pan and set aside to rest.

Add the beans to the pan with the reserved oil and fry for a few minutes, then roughly crush with a fork. Season well, drizzle with extra-virgin olive oil and serve with the rested pork chops and the piperrada.

At the table

SAUTÉED PEAS WITH CHORIZO MIGAS & GOLDEN FRIED EGG

Serves 6

olive oil
2 banana shallots (echalions), finely
    chopped
2 garlic cloves, finely chopped
400 g (14 oz) fresh baby peas
125 g (4 oz) cooking chorizo, cut into
    small cubes
150 g (5 oz) stale bread, cut into
    small cubes
sea salt and freshly ground black
    pepper
6 free-range eggs
handful of mint leaves

If you are lucky enough to try *guisantes de lágrima* (peas of tears) in the Basque, then you will surely agree that these are the best peas ever. I believe they got this name simply because they are very small. It's true, they are really tiny, with an unforgettable sweet flavour. So few are produced that they can exceed the price of gold! Don't miss the harvest, which runs from March to June.

I think this dish is perfect at any time – for breakfast, lunch or dinner. Proper comfort food!

Heat a little oil in a pan and gently fry the shallots and garlic for a few minutes. Add the peas and a little splash of water and sauté gently until tender.

Meanwhile, fry the chorizo in a separate pan with a little oil. Once it has started to turn golden and has released all its fat, remove with a slotted spoon and set aside. Add the bread cubes to the chorizo oil and fry until crisp. Put the chorizo back into the pan, mix together and season.

Heat a good layer of oil in a non-stick frying pan and fry the eggs, so that the whites bubble up and go crispy but the yolks stay soft.

Serve the sautéed peas and bread cubes with the chorizo migas, scatter with mint and top with the crispy golden egg. Serve immediately.

FISH

Basque people love fresh fish and seafood, as do I.

Basque people love fresh fish and seafood, as do I. With the Cantabrian Sea on the doorstep, fishing has always been a big part of the Basque economy. Fishermen go out to bring the catch in so that the women can sell it at the fish markets and fishing was, and still is, at the heart of the lives of many families in the region.

Some of the recipes you'll see in this chapter come literally off the boats. Dishes that the fishermen would cook whilst out at sea for sustenance, such as the Marmitako. Others come straight from the *sociedades gastronómicas*, where traditionally only men used to cook and they would prepare the catch.

Others are some of my favourite recipes, recipes that bring me great memories of really early mornings at the markets, memories of chatting with the old lady cleaning the anchovies. It's amazing to see how much love still goes into this task, day after day.

There's so much to say about fish and how it fits into life in the Basque Country. From drinking Txakoli and eating fresh sardines *a la plancha* down in the port of San Sebastián to salt cod, a staple of many dishes that you will see across the bars and restaurants of the region.

In this chapter I also want to show you that you don't need to be scared of fish – buying it, preparing it or cooking it. These recipes are meant to be made at home and with fish that you will be able to find in your local supermarkets or at your fishmonger.

Pintxo

TUNA CONFIT WITH GUINDILLAS, ANCHOVY & WHITE ONION (INDURAIN)

Makes 6 pintxos (with tuna confit to spare)

6 salted anchovies
30 pickled guindillas or 18 large
  ones, halved
6 small pieces of white onion
6 pitted manzanilla olives
extra-virgin olive oil to drizzle

for the tuna confit
750 ml (25 fl oz) olive oil
pared zest of 1 orange and 1 lemon
few sprigs each of marjoram and
  thyme
10 black peppercorns
900 g (2 lb) bonito tuna loin cut into
  pieces, approximately 5 cm (2 in)
  long, 4 cm (1½ in) wide and 2 cm
  (1 in) thick (ask a good fishmonger)

This is the interpretation of the famous *gilda* from restaurant Bodega Donostiarra, where they add tuna confit and some raw onion.

The story with this dish is that you should eat it in one bite. It's big, so you need be a champion to eat it! A champion like cyclist Miguel 'Big Mig' Indurain, the first Spaniard to win the Tour de France in 1991, who the dish is named after. This pintxo is made from five guindillas – representing the five tours Indurain won – and it's one of the bestselling.

First make the tuna confit. Put the oil in a pan with the orange and lemon zests, the herbs and peppercorns. Heat the oil until it reaches 140–150°C (285–300°F). Remove from the heat and let it cool almost right down.

Slip the tuna into the barely warm oil, then return to the heat and bring back to 100°C (210°F). Take off the heat and allow the tuna to confit in the cooling oil. Test it after a few minutes to see if it is cooked – it should still be just a tiny bit pink in the middle when flaked.

Remove the tuna from the oil and put in a plastic container. Let the oil cool, then pour over the tuna and it will keep in the fridge for 2 weeks.

For the pintxos, take six small pieces of the tuna (keep the rest for other recipes). Top each piece with a salted anchovy, five guindillas, a piece of onion and an olive. Secure with a cocktail stick, if you like, and drizzle with plenty of extra-virgin olive oil before serving.

At the table

ROAST JOHN DORY, ALUBIAS DE TOLOSA & PANCETTA

Serves 4

1 quantity of alubias de Tolosa
    (see page 190)
200 g (7 oz) waxy potatoes, sliced
1 bulb garlic, cloves separated
2 kg (4½ lb) John Dory
olive oil to drizzle
sea salt and freshly ground black
    pepper
150 g (5 oz) pancetta, very finely
    chopped

I visit Wales regularly to visit my close friends and family in Cardiff, and quite often we head straight to my favourite fishmonger as soon as I arrive. My eyes are always drawn to the gorgeous, but at the same time ugly, John Dory; it looks at me and says 'cook me'! Once I bought one that was almost two kilos (over four pounds) – the fishmonger thought I was crazy (which I am), but after a very long lunch two of us finished the whole fish! The creaminess of the Tolosa beans makes them the perfect match for this dish.

Cook the beans according to the recipe. When almost cooked, preheat the oven to 180°C (350°F /Gas 3).

Scatter the potatoes and garlic in the bottom of a large roasting tin. Place the John Dory on top, drizzle with plenty of olive oil and season well. Roast for 30–40 minutes until just cooked. Test by inserting a sharp knife into the flesh; when it pulls away from the bone easily, it's done.

Meanwhile, fry the pancetta in a dry pan until crispy. Serve the John Dory, potatoes and garlic with the cooked beans scattered with the crispy pancetta.

Pintxo

GRILLED OCTOPUS WITH PEPPERS & AUBERGINE

Serves 6–8

1 carrot, peeled and roughly chopped
1 onion, roughly chopped
1 celery stalk, chopped
1 bay leaf
8 black peppercorns
400 g (14 oz) large fresh octopus tentacles, cleaned (ask a good fishmonger)
1 aubergine (eggplant), cut into pieces
1 red pepper, deseeded and cut into pieces
1 green pepper, deseeded and cut into pieces
75–100 ml (2½–3½ fl oz) olive oil plus extra to drizzle
sea salt and freshly ground black pepper
large handful of parsley

I always get asked how to cook tender octopus. Of course the important thing is always to buy good-quality octopus and then cook it properly. I do have a secret, though, and that is to freeze the octopus for a minimum of two days before cooking. This breaks down the fibres and makes it much more delicate.

Bring a pan of water to the boil with the carrot, onion, celery, bay leaf and peppercorns. Plunge the octopus tentacles into the water and simmer for 50–60 minutes. Drain and slice on the diagonal into pieces 1 cm (½ in) thick.

Meanwhile, preheat the oven to 190°C (375°F/Gas 5).

Put the aubergine and peppers in a roasting tin and drizzle with plenty of oil. Season and roast for 30–40 minutes until really tender.

Blanch the parsley in boiling water for 30 seconds, then plunge into a bowl of iced water. Whizz in a processor with the olive oil until you have a lovely green oil. Push through a fine sieve into a bowl. Season and set aside.

Toss the octopus in a little oil. Heat a heavy-based pan or chargrill pan over a high heat and, when really hot, sear the octopus for 2–3 minutes, turning once.

Serve the octopus with the roasted vegetables and a good drizzle of the parsley oil.

SEAFOOD SALAD WITH MANGO & CHILLI DRESSING

Serves 6

600 g (1 lb 5 oz) fresh whole squid, cleaned (ask a good fishmonger)
18 small raw shell-on prawns
18 fresh queenie scallops
olive oil
300 g (10½ oz) fresh palourde clams, cleaned

for the dressing
1 small mango
1 red chilli, deseeded and finely chopped
zest of 1 and juice of 2 limes
5 tablespoons extra-virgin olive oil
handful of chopped coriander (cilantro)
sea salt and freshly ground black pepper

Seafood salad is called *salpicón de marisco* in Spain and you can use as many different types of seafood as you can get in the market that day.

I had a similar dish in a bar near San Sebastián, and when I saw it on the menu I wasn't particularly sure about it, so obviously I had to order it. I have to say that the flavours worked so well; the hit from the chilli, the sweetness of the fruit and the saltiness and sweetness of the seafood are a perfect combination.

Cut the body of the squid into squares and score in a crisscross pattern with a very sharp knife, being careful not to slice all the way through. Slice the tentacles into lengths. Toss all the seafood, except the clams, in olive oil.

Make the dressing. Finely chop the flesh of the mango and mix with the rest of the ingredients, season well and set aside.

Heat a large heavy-based frying pan or chargrill pan over a high heat. Cook the squid and octopus first, for a couple of minutes, turning, until tender, then remove to a serving dish.

Add the prawns to the pan and cook, turning, until they have turned pink. Add to the squid. Next cook the scallops for a minute, then turn and cook for a minute more until golden but just cooked. Add to the dish.

Finally cook the clams. Tip into the pan and cover with a lid (or use a baking sheet) and allow to steam open (discard any clams that refuse to open). Tip into the serving dish, toss together with the dressing and serve warm.

At the table

SCALLOPS, SAUTÉED CABBAGE & MORCILLA

Serves 4

olive oil
2 garlic cloves , finely chopped
1 savoy cabbage, finely chopped
sea salt and freshly ground black
    pepper
250 g (9 oz) morcilla, cut into 12–16
    slices 1 cm (½ in) thick
12–16 fresh king scallops with roe

When we were shooting the pictures for this book, I was looking around the market for a really good cabbage because I know they grow really amazing ones in the Basque Country. Scallops and morcilla are two of my favourite ingredients, so I experimented by adding some of the lovely sweet cabbage that I'd found, and there you have it!

Heat a little oil in a pan and fry the garlic for 30 seconds, then add the cabbage and a few tablespoons of water. Cover and cook slowly for 20–30 minutes until really tender, stirring occasionally. Uncover, season, and cook for a few minutes more.

Meanwhile, heat a little more oil in a heavy-based pan over a high heat and fry the morcilla until crispy on both sides. Crumble the morcilla and set aside. Brush the scallops with oil and fry for 1–2 minutes each side until golden and just cooked.

Serve the scallops on a bed of the cabbage with the crispy morcilla scattered over.

At the table

SARDINES MARINATED IN CIDER OR TXAKOLI VINEGAR

Serves 4

1 bulb garlic
olive oil
500 ml (17 fl oz) Txakoli or cider
    vinegar
1 small French shallot, finely
    chopped
5 black peppercorns
5 pink peppercorns
1 bay leaf
few sprigs of tarragon
25 g (1 oz) caster (superfine) sugar
8 super-fresh sardines, filleted
toasted baguette to serve
extra-virgin olive oil to drizzle
flaky sea salt

My love of sardines goes back as far as I can remember. My mum used to come home from the market every Tuesday with sardines in her bag. That strong fresh fish flavour will stay with me forever, as will a glass of fresh milk straight from the cow.

The simplest way to prepare sardines is to remove the scales, fillet them, then eat them raw. I wanted to give some extra flavour to this dish, as not many people will eat them raw.

This marinade is very quick, which means you will keep almost all of the flavour as well as the freshness of the fish.

Preheat the oven to 170°C (340°F/Gas 3).

Drizzle the garlic with oil and roast for 30–40 minutes until really tender. Squeeze the pulp from the skins and mash into a paste. Set aside.

Gently heat the vinegar with the shallot, peppercorns, herbs and sugar until the sugar has dissolved, but not until it boils. Lay the sardines skin side down in a dish and pour over the hot vinegar. Leave for a couple of minutes, then drain.

Spread the toasted baguette with some of the garlic paste. Top with the marinated sardines, drizzle with extra-virgin olive oil and sprinkle with the flaky sea salt.

Pintxo

TORTILLA DE BACALAO

Serves 4–6

400 g (14 oz) salt cod
125 ml (4 fl oz) olive oil
3 large white onions, finely sliced
handful of thyme, leaves stripped
6 free-range eggs
freshly ground black pepper
handful of finely chopped flat-leaf
   parsley

Another *tortilla de bacalao*? Well yes, I couldn't write a book on the food of the Basque Country and not include this recipe. It's a must-have dish when you are in a *sidrería* (cider house).

My interpretation is to caramelise the onions to bring more sweetness to the tortilla and the *bacalao* is not cooked.

When you caramelise the onions, make plenty as you can keep them in the fridge for at least a week – they make a great addition to any sandwich, or just on toast with some goat's cheese. Heaven.

Soak the cod in cold water, skin side up, for 24 hours, changing the water a couple of times.

Heat the oil in a large pan and gently fry the onions for a few minutes. Cover with a lid and cook over a low heat for 25 minutes until really soft. Remove the lid, add the thyme and cook for a further 20–25 minutes until really caramelised and sticky. Scoop out with a slotted spoon, keeping some of the oil, and cool.

Remove the skin from the cod and flake into large pieces.

Beat the eggs with plenty of black pepper and gently fold in the onion, cod and parsley.

In a large (23 cm/9 in) non-stick pan, heat 2–3 tablespoons of the reserved oil and pour in the egg mixture. Swirl the pan over a high heat until the mixture starts to set around the edges, then reduce the heat and cook for 4–5 minutes until it just starts to set, so that the bottom and sides are golden but it is still quite loose in the middle.

Cover the pan with a flat lid or board, turn the tortilla carefully onto it, then put the pan back on a low heat. Return the tortilla to the pan, cooked side up, and use a spatula to tuck the edges of the tortilla under to give its characteristic curved look. Cook for a couple of minutes, then turn onto a board and serve. It should still be lovely and juicy when you cut into it.

At the table

MERLUZA EN SALSA VERDE

Serves 4

3 tablespoons olive oil
3 garlic cloves
1 small shallot, finely chopped
1 tablespoon plain (all-purpose) flour
200 ml (7 fl oz) Txakoli or other crisp
   dry white wine
150 ml fresh fish stock
4 × 180g hake fillets
sea salt and finely ground black
   pepper
200g (7 oz) peas
200g (7 oz) fresh clams, cleaned
8 (or 4 large) white asparagus,
   blanched for 5–8 minutes
1 small handful of finely chopped
   parsley

I've been so lucky to have been able to cook this dish in one of the *sociedades gastronómicas* or *txoko* (gastronomic societies). It was a great feeling to see the men cooking for the women, turning a long-held tradition on its head, as for a long time women weren't allowed into the *sociedades*.

This is a very popular dish in Basque cooking, I have cooked the white asparagus as per the recipe on page 169, but in Spain they normally use tinned asparagus. For the peas, many people blanch beforehand, but I just add them to the sauce and allow them to cook for a couple of minutes in there.

In the Basque kitchen, a very similar recipe to this is *merluza a la Koxkera*, which is almost exactly the same except it uses green asparagus.

It is almost impossible to get into a *sociedad gastronómica*, but you can eat this recipe at the restaurant Bodegón Alejandro, where you will find many of the local dishes cooked to perfection.

Heat the olive oil in a frying pan over a medium heat and fry the garlic and the shallot until soft and lightly golden – this will take around 3–4 minutes. Add the flour and cook for about 2 minutes, then slowly add the wine and cook for another 2 minutes before adding the stock. You should then have a silky-smooth sauce.

Season the hake fillets and add to the sauce. Cook the hake for 4–5 minutes, then add the peas and clams, cover and cook for 2–3 minutes until the clams open. Discard any clams that do no open. To finish, add the asparagus and parsley, keep simmering for a minute, season to taste and serve with some crusty bread.

BACALAO A LA VIZCAINA

Serves 4

800 g (1 lb 12 oz) salt cod
3 tablespoons olive oil
1 large onion, finely chopped
2 garlic cloves, sliced
2 tomatoes, finely chopped
5 large red (bell) peppers
150 ml (5 fl oz) white wine

Bacalao salao is the true name for salt cod in Spanish, but it is always shortened to just *bacalao* (cod) or *bakailao* in Basque.

Preserving food by drying has been a popular method for a long time. When we dry cod with salt, it doesn't just preserve the fish but adds sweetness and saltiness at the same time. Always use *bacalao* that's a gorgeous silvery white in colour; if it's yellow, it means that it's bad quality.

This recipe is one of the most popular dishes from the Basque kitchen. If you can cook the peppers over charcoal it will add a deeper flavour to the sauce; if not, then grill them instead.

Soak the cod in cold water, skin side up, for 24 hours, changing the water a couple of times.

In a saucepan, heat 2 tablespoons of the oil, add the onion and slowly cook until it turns transparent. Add the garlic and cook for 3 minutes. Then add the tomatoes and cook for another 4–5 minutes until the juices from the tomatoes evaporate.

Using a blowtorch or under a very hot grill (broiler), blacken the pepper skins all over. Put into a freezer bag, seal and stand for 5 minutes to steam. Remove the skins from the peppers. Halve and discard the seeds, then finely slice. Add the peppers and the wine to the saucepan and cook over a low heat for 15 minutes (I like a crunchy sauce).

Cut the cod into four pieces. In a frying pan, heat the remaining tablespoon of oil over a medium heat. Add the cod, skin side down, and cook for 4 minutes, then turn over and cook for another 4 minutes, depending on the thickness of the fish, until it is almost ready (you want to finish the cooking in the sauce).

When the fish is almost ready, put into the sauce and cook for another 3 minutes until just cooked.

At the table
MACKEREL MARMITAKO

Serves 4

olive oil
1 large onion, finely sliced
2 garlic cloves, crushed
1 red (bell) pepper, deseeded
 and thinly sliced
1 green (bell) pepper, deseeded
 and thinly sliced
1 bay leaf
1 tablespoon choricero paste
 or pimentón
750 g (1 lb 10 oz) floury potatoes,
 peeled
500 ml (17 fl oz) fresh fish or
 vegetable stock
sea salt and freshly ground black
 pepper
4 fresh mackerel, filleted

Writing a book about Basque cuisine and not including a *marmitako* would not be right. I love the original version with tuna, but when you make the base of the potato stew and finish with some mackerel *a la plancha* on top, it takes the traditional recipe to a whole different level.

***Marmitako* was a typical meal for the Basque fishermen and was normally cooked for when they were in their boats. The name is taken from the Spanish word *marmite*, meaning pot.**

Heat a good layer of olive oil in a large pan with a lid and gently fry the onion for 5 minutes, then add the garlic, pepper slices and bay leaf. Cover and cook for 10–15 minutes until really soft. Add the choricero paste or pimentón and cook for a minute.

Use the point of a knife to break the potatoes into pieces (you don't want to chop them as you need the rough surface to make a good thick stew). Tip the potatoes into the pan and pour over the stock to cover. Season and cook with the lid on for around 20–30 minutes until the potatoes are starting to break down. Remove the lid and bubble for a further 10 minutes.

Season the mackerel and rub with oil. Heat a heavy-based frying pan over a high heat and fry the mackerel, skin side down, for a couple of minutes until almost cooked. Flip over for 30 seconds and then remove from the pan.

Spoon the *marmitako* into warmed bowls, top with the mackerel and serve.

At the table

SAUTÉED CLAMS WITH GARLIC, LEMON & PARSLEY

Serves 4

olive oil
3 fat garlic cloves, peeled and finely
    sliced
1 lemon, half finely sliced, half juiced
1 kg (2 lb 3 oz) fresh palourde clams,
    cleaned
few sprigs of thyme, leaves stripped
handful of finely chopped flat-leaf
    parsley

Clams are popular all over the world as they are so versatile. When you are planning to cook for more than a couple of people, this is something that you must consider; ingredients and dishes your friends will love but are also quick prepare, so that you don't spend the whole time at the stove.

You can boil some pasta with this for a really easy lunch, and add some chilli for an extra kick.

Heat a little oil in a deep heavy-based stockpot. Fry the garlic and lemon slices for 30 seconds, then increase the heat to high, tip in all the clams and cover with a lid. Cook for 2–3 minutes, shaking the pan occasionally, until the clams have all opened (discard any that refuse to open).

Add the lemon juice and herbs and serve with lots of crusty bread to mop up the juices.

Pintxo

COD TONGUE WITH SAUTÉED RED CABBAGE & CIDER VINEGAR

Serves 4

olive oil
1 French shallot, finely sliced
1 garlic clove, finely chopped
good pinch of chilli flakes
½ red cabbage (about 500 g/1 lb 2 oz),
    very finely sliced
100 ml (3½ fl oz) cider vinegar
sea salt and freshly ground black
    pepper
16 small super-fresh cod tongues,
    trimmed

In Spain we call cod tongues *kokotxas de bacalao* – to be honest, I don't know why they're called tongues because they're not really, but are in fact the lower part of the fish head. Hake tongues are very popular all over Spain. In the UK, cod tongues will be much easier to find, so give this recipe a try as they are just delicious; so tender and silky in your mouth. I love them just grilled.

These are definitely a delicacy for me and if you are lucky enough to get a small one, be sure to eat it all in one go.

Heat a little oil in a large pan and gently fry the shallot for a few minutes, then add the garlic and chilli flakes. Fry for 30 seconds, then add the cabbage and sauté for 10–12 minutes until tender but still with a crunch. Add the cider vinegar and bubble for a few minutes. Season and set aside.

Toss the cod tongues in a little oil and season. Light a small barbecue or heat a heavy-based frying pan over a high heat and quickly sear the tongues for 4–5 minutes, turning once, until just cooked. You can tell they are cooked as the meat inside the skin will change to opaque white. Serve with the cabbage.

At the table

BACALAO AL PIL-PIL

Serves 4

4 pieces of salt cod, 150 g (5 oz) each
1 dried chilli
100 ml (3½ fl oz) extra-virgin olive oil
6 garlic cloves, sliced
handful of chopped parsley

Pil-pil is an emulsion made from the gelatine of the fish and the infused oil – it may sound unusual, but it's heavenly. It's not an easy one to do, but it will make you happy when you're eating it, so I think it's worth it.

The important thing here is that you keep the temperature of the oil at around 80°C (175°F). You may also need to add cold water to the gelatine to help the emulsion to mix properly.

Soak the cod in cold water, skin side up, for 24 hours, changing the water a couple of times.

The next day, check that the cod is desalted, choosing a bit from the inside, then remove any bones and dry properly.

Clean the chilli inside by taking out all the seeds, put in water to rehydrate and slice into small rings. Heat the oil in a terracotta dish or a heavy-based pan big enough to accommodate the pieces of fish. Over a medium heat, fry the garlic and chilli until golden, then remove from the oil and reserve.

Place the cod pieces in the oil with the skin up and cook over a medium-low heat, never frying. When you can see the gelatine coming out of the fish, turn over and cook for a bit longer. The total cooking time for the fish should be about 20 minutes. When the fish is cooked, take out and set aside in a warm place.

Take the terracotta dish off the heat and leave to cool a little. When the oil is around 80°C (175°F), use a small whisk to whisk the gelatine by making constant circular motions. You should get a nice thick and silky emulsion.

Put the cod back into the sauce, followed by the garlic and chilli. Garnish with the parsley and eat hot.

At the table

PAN-FRIED HAKE WITH SAUTÉED WILD CHANTERELLES & SAGE

Serves 4

olive oil
2 French shallots, finely chopped
2 garlic cloves, crushed
few small sage leaves
300 g (10½ oz) chanterelles, cleaned
100 ml (3½ fl oz) fresh fish stock
sea salt and freshly ground black
    pepper
4 hake fillets (175 g/6 oz each)

Hake is one of the most sought-after fish in the Basque Country. I really don't know why it's not as popular here in the UK, particularly as it's plentiful – I think most of the catch from the sea here goes to Spain!

In my family, our favourite way of cooking hake is *a la romana*, or Roman style, which means that it's battered.

In this recipe, I bring two big flavours together, the sage and the mushrooms, but they complement the fish very well.

Heat a little olive oil in a pan and gently fry the shallots for 5–10 minutes until really soft. Add the garlic and sage and cook for 30 seconds, then increase the heat and add the mushrooms. Fry for 45 minutes, then add the stock and bubble for a couple of minutes. Season and set aside.

Heat a heavy-based frying pan with a little bit of oil. Add the hake skin side down and cook for 4–5 minutes until almost cooked through. Flip over and cook for 30 seconds more.

Put the cooked hake, skin side up, into the pan with the mushrooms. Cook for a minute or two more, then serve.

Pintxo

CHARRED BABY GEM WITH PIQUILLO PEPPERS, SALTED ANCHOVIES & BLUE CHEESE

Serves 4

50 g (2 oz) piquillo peppers, drained
extra-virgin olive oil
pinch of dried oregano
sea salt and freshly ground black
    pepper
1 red onion, very finely sliced
2 baby gem lettuces, halved
    lengthways
olive oil
100 g (3½ oz) Basque blue cheese
    or Roquefort
8 salted anchovies

Anchovies can come in so many different guises and I really can't decide which is my favourite. I like to enjoy them fried with a small glass of beer or *zurito*, as the Basque people call it; salted just on their own with some cider; and the white ones are delicious with a local Txakoli. All of them are great, and, as you can tell, make the perfect accompaniment if you have a drink in hand, which is why they are always on the menu in any bar.

Maybe you don't think of 'salad' as a pintxo, but I can assure you that using baby gem as a sort of 'cup' makes them the perfect finger food.

Finely slice the piquillo peppers and toss with extra-virgin olive oil, the oregano and seasoning and set aside.

Put the red onion in a bowl, cover with cold water and stand for 10 minutes. Drain, pat dry and toss with a little extra-virgin olive oil and plenty of salt and pepper.

Rub the cut side of the baby gem with olive oil. Heat a heavy-based pan over a high heat and cook the lettuce, cut side down, for a couple of minutes until charred. Flip over and cook for a minute more, then place on a serving plate.

Top each of the charred baby gem with some of the piquillo peppers, scatter over the blue cheese and finish off each one with two anchovies. Sprinkle over the red onion and serve.

Pintxo

RUSSIAN SALAD WITH PRAWNS

Serves 4

500 g (1 lb 2 oz) waxy potatoes,
    cut into bite-sized pieces
2 carrots, peeled and diced
150 g (5 oz) peas, fresh or frozen
25 g (1 oz) piquillo peppers, drained
    and finely chopped
16 slices of baguette
1 hard-boiled free-range egg, peeled
2 tablespoons finely chopped
    parsley
16 small prawns/crevettes (shell-on
    shrimp), cooked and peeled

for the lemon mayonnaise
2 free-range egg yolks, at room
    temperature
zest and juice of 1 lemon
sea salt and freshly ground black
    pepper
200 ml (7 fl oz) sunflower oil
100 ml (3½ fl oz) olive oil

This is a great pintxo and perfect for a party or if you're cooking for a group. It's really easy to prepare the ingredients the morning or evening before, and assemble just before your guests arrive.

Make the lemon mayonnaise first. Put the egg yolks in a bowl with the lemon zest, a small squeeze of juice and plenty of seasoning. Whisk together, then very gradually whisk in the oils, in a thin steady stream, until you have a thick, glossy mayonnaise. Add lemon juice to taste and set aside.

Cook the potatoes in a pan of boiling salted water for 10 minutes until tender. Add the carrots and peas for the last few minutes, then drain and tip into a bowl.

Add the piquillo peppers and enough of the mayonnaise to bind together (about half – the rest can be kept in the fridge for up to a week).

Toast the baguette slices and top with the potato salad. Grate the egg and scatter over the top together with the parsley. Finish each one with a prawn and serve.

At the table
SQUID IN INK

Serves 4–6

olive oil
2 large onions, julienned
1 garlic clove, sliced
1 tomato, finely chopped
2 sachets of squid ink
175 ml (6 fl oz) Txakoli or other crisp
    dry white wine
500 g (1 lb 2 oz) squid (or 250 g/9 oz
    cleaned squid)
sea salt

Sitting in the port of San Sebastián looking at the boats, people-watching as children jump in and out of the sea, and enjoying a plate of squid in ink and a cold beer is heaven for me.

In Spanish we call this dish *chipirones en su tinta* and you will quite often find it in tins. The first time I had the proper ones, I was in my twenties, and it's that first taste of the real thing still sticks in my memory. I still love the tinned version though as it reminds me of my childhood.

Heat a little olive oil in a pan and gently fry the onions for 5 minutes until they are beginning to soften.

Next, add the sliced garlic and tomato and cook over a medium heat for 5–10 minutes.

In a separate bowl, mix the squid ink with the wine. Add this to the tomatoes and boil for 30 minutes.

Cool the mixture slightly and blitz in a food processor until you have a creamy sauce without lumps. Check the seasoning, then add the squid. Simmer for 15–20 minutes and serve in warm bowls with some crusty bread.

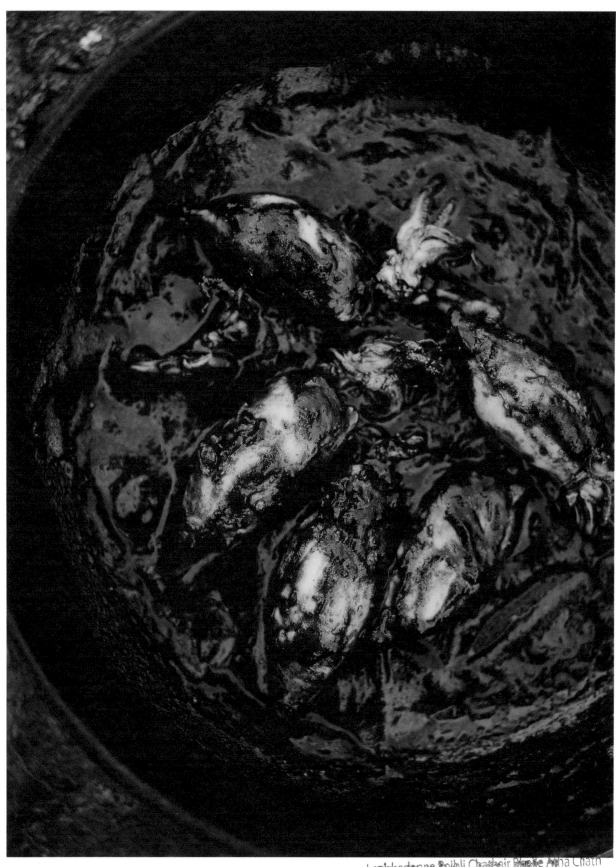

Pintxo

SARDINES A LA PLANCHA

Serves 4

16–20 really fresh sardines
sea salt and freshly ground black
    pepper
olive oil for brushing
extra-virgin olive oil to drizzle
flaky sea salt
lemon wedges to serve

Sardines *a la plancha* are something that Spanish people prefer to eat out and I can agree in some ways, as the smell can linger if you don't have a well-ventilated kitchen! I think they're definitely worth it, though. You can barbecue them as well, which I love as it gives the flesh a sort of bitter flavour, which is delicious – just add some olive oil and lemon juice for the perfect finish.

If you are lucky enough to be in the port at San Sebastián, go to the restaurant Mariñela and enjoy a plate of these beauties – they really know how to cook them.

Scale the sardines under cold water using your fingertips to pull and scratch them away. Pat dry, season and brush with olive oil.

Heat a barbecue, heavy-based pan or chargrill pan over a high heat. Cook the sardines for a couple of minutes, turning once, until charred and just cooked through.

Remove the sardines and serve with a drizzle of extra-virgin olive oil, a scattering of flaky sea salt, a squeeze of lemon and some crusty bread.

Pintxo

GAMBAS A LA PLANCHA

Serves 4

fine sea salt to scatter
16–20 prawns (shell-on shrimp)
olive oil for brushing
extra-virgin olive oil to drizzle
lemon wedges to serve

The first thing I tell people to do when eating prawns is to suck the head. They think I'm crazy at first, but they never regret doing it as this is without doubt the part with the most flavour. I like to describe a prawn as a cocktail of sea flavours: first eat the head then the tail; the tail will have a totally different flavour, it's much sweeter.

Heat a barbecue, heavy-based pan or chargrill pan over a high heat and scatter with a good handful of sea salt. Brush the prawns with olive oil and cook for a minute or two, turning once, until they have just turned pinky.

Serve with a drizzle of extra-virgin olive oil, lemon wedges and perhaps some crusty bread.

Pintxo

SARDINE, BOILED EGG & CAPER EMPANADAS

Serves 6

olive oil
1 onion, finely chopped
1 red (bell) pepper, deseeded and
 finely sliced
1 green (bell) pepper, deseeded and
 finely sliced
118 g (4 oz) tin of sardines, such as
 La Brújula, drained and roughly
 chopped
2 hard-boiled free-range eggs,
 roughly chopped
1 tablespoon small capers, rinsed,
 squeezed dry and chopped
handful of finely chopped parsley

for the pastry
500 g (1 lb 2 oz) plain (all-purpose)
 flour
1 teaspoon fine sea salt
200 g (7 oz) cold unsalted butter,
 cut into cubes
1 free-range egg
75 ml (2½ fl oz) cold water
2 teaspoons white wine vinegar
1 free-range egg yolk, beaten,
 to glaze

I can't get enough of these pastries. This is the recipe that my mum taught me, originally using tinned tuna. They are delicious if you want to stick with tinned tuna, but you should also try them with the tuna confit from page 78 or with sardines, which is how I now like to make them. Get the tin with little sardines called *sardinillas* if you can, as these are the best.

Make the pastry first. Tip the flour and salt into a bowl and rub the butter in with your fingertips until it looks like breadcrumbs. Mix the egg with the cold water and vinegar, add to the bowl and mix in quickly with a flat knife. Bring together with your hands and knead briefly until smooth, then shape into a disc, wrap in cling film (plastic wrap) and chill for at least 30 minutes.

Heat a little oil in a pan and gently fry the onion and peppers for 10–15 minutes until softened and tender. Tip into a bowl and mix with the sardines, eggs, capers and parsley. Allow to cool.

Preheat the oven to 200°C (400°F/Gas 6).

Divide the dough into 24 even-sized pieces and place under a damp tea towel (dish towel) to stop them drying out. One at a time, roll them out on a lightly floured surface until they are 10 cm (4 in) in diameter. Place a spoonful of the sardine mixture into the centre of one half of the circle. Brush the edge with the beaten egg yolk, then fold over and crimp with your fingers.

Place on a lined baking sheet and repeat with the rest of the dough and filling.

Brush the empanadas all over with the beaten egg and bake for 25–30 minutes until golden. Cool a little and serve.

Pintxo

GORDAL OLIVES STUFFED WITH WHITE ANCHOVIES

Makes 14–16 pintxos

14–16 boquerones
150 g (5 oz) pitted gordal olives, drained
extra-virgin olive oil
sea salt and freshly ground black pepper

Manzanilla olives stuffed with anchovies has long been a winning combination, and is a staple at many a tapas bar. I love gordal olives as well, though, and have chosen them here, with the added twist of using *boquerones* or white anchovies. I think this works very well, as the *boquerones* are really sweet and with the addition of olive oil and the salt, all of the flavours come together nicely.

It can be confusing when we talk about *boquerones* and anchovies – the difference actually lies in the way that they've been preserved or cured, as otherwise they are the same fish. *Boquerones* are cured in vinegar and are very often called 'white anchovies', whereas regular anchovies are cured and preserved in salt until they are filleted and put into a tin with olive oil.

Roll up each of the *boquerones* so that they fit inside an olive. Stuff all of the olives, then drizzle with extra-virgin olive oil and season with the sea salt and black pepper.

Pintxo

SQUID MEATBALLS WITH SAFFRON & ALMOND SAUCE

Serves 4

600 g (1 lb 5 oz) fresh squid, cleaned
1 red chilli, finely chopped
1 garlic clove, finely chopped
50–75 g (2–2½ oz) dry breadcrumbs
handful of coriander (cilantro), finely
    chopped
1 free-range egg
sea salt and white pepper
plain (all-purpose) flour for dusting
olive oil for frying
chopped parsley for garnish

for the sauce
2 tablespoons olive oil
1 banana shallot (echalion), finely
    chopped
1 small onion, finely chopped
1 garlic clove, crushed
5–6 ripe tomatoes, skins and seeds
    removed
750 ml (25 fl oz) fresh fish stock
good pinch of saffron
50 g (2 oz) ground almonds
sea salt and freshly ground black
    pepper

I took inspiration for this recipe from the traditional *albóndigas* **that you'll always see in tapas bars and from the Ibérico pork meatballs that we serve with a cuttlefish sauce at my restaurants – but I have made the squid the star here.**

The most important thing to remember when serving squid or cuttlefish is to cook it either very quickly or very slowly, otherwise it becomes tough and chewy. For this recipe, I've cooked it quickly, to ensure it's really tender.

Finely chop the squid and mix with the chilli, garlic, breadcrumbs, coriander and egg. Season well with the sea salt and white pepper. Lightly oil your hands and roll the mixture into small balls, about 30 g (1 oz) each. Chill in the fridge while you make the sauce.

Heat the oil in a pan and gently fry the shallot and onion for 10 minutes until lovely and soft. Add the garlic and cook for a minute more, then add the tomatoes and stock and simmer for 20 minutes to reduce to a thick sauce.

Soak the saffron in 2 tablespoons hot water for a few minutes, then mix with the ground almonds to form a paste and add to the pan with plenty of seasoning. Simmer for 5 minutes to thicken. Set aside.

Dust the squid in flour. Heat a good amount of oil in a non-stick pan and fry the squid for 2–3 minutes, turning until golden brown. Drain on paper towels.

Add the squid meatballs to the sauce and heat through gently, then scatter with parsley and serve.

PINTXO OF CRAB & PRAWNS

Makes 20 pintxos

100 g (3½ oz) brown crab meat
300 g (10½ oz) white crab meat
2 hard-boiled free-range eggs, grated
40 small cooked Atlantic prawns (shrimp)
parsley leaves for garnish

for the pastry
265 g (9½ oz) plain (all-purpose) flour
110 g (3¾ oz) unsalted butter
pinch of sea salt
2–3 tablespoons cold water

for the mayonnaise
2 free-range egg yolks
good squeeze of lemon juice
good pinch of sea salt and freshly ground black pepper
150 ml (5 fl oz) rapeseed, groundnut (peanut) or sunflower oil
150 ml (5 fl oz) light olive oil

You can't and you shouldn't miss this when visiting restaurant Ganbara, located in the heart of the old town in San Sebastián. When Amaia sees me coming, she always prepares some of this and a glass of Txakoli – in my eyes this is the perfect welcome.

You can make the pastry the day before, then just prepare the filling the next day when you're ready. In this recipe I do prefer to use a light olive oil in the mayonnaise to ensure that the crab is the main flavour.

For the pastry, rub the flour and butter together with your fingers until it resembles breadcrumbs, then add the salt and enough cold water to bring together with your hands. Knead briefly then shape into a disc and wrap in cling film (plastic wrap) and chill for 30 minutes.

Put the egg yolks in a bowl with a squeeze of lemon juice and some seasoning. Very slowly whisk in the rapeseed and olive oils until you have a thick, glossy mayonnaise. Add a little more lemon juice to taste.

Preheat the oven to 200°C (400°F/Gas 6). Roll out the pastry on a floured surface until 2–3 mm (⅛ in) thick and cut out 6 cm (2½ in) discs with a cookie cutter, rerolling the trimmings, and use to line 20 holes of a 7 cm (2¾ in) muffin tin. Bake for 8–10 minutes until lightly golden and crisp then allow to cool on a wire rack.

Combine the brown and white crab meats with two thirds of the mayonnaise. Spoon the crab meat mix into the cooked tart case. Dollop on a little more mayonnaise and sprinkle over the grated egg. Top each tart with two prawns, garnish with a parsley leaf and serve.

At the table

CREAMED RICE WITH CUTTLEFISH & PRAWNS

Cuttlefish is popular all over Spain and can be cooked in many different ways: quickly on a very hot plancha just with some lemon and mayonnaise is heaven; or battered with some flour and then quickly deep-fried is delicious, too.

This is a recipe where you have to cook the cuttlefish for a long time to make it really tender. I think this is the perfect comforting supper for a cold winter's evening, best enjoyed served in a big bowl as you sit by the fire. It's one I often cook for friends and is the original 'one-pot wonder'.

And proof that you never stop learning – once when I was cooking this dish, I added a big splash of Txakoli to the pot just because I was drinking some at the time. It brought a whole new freshness to the dish, which I loved, and now I do this whenever I have a bottle open. Don't worry if you don't have any, though; a good dry white wine will do just as well.

Serves 4–6

olive oil

1 banana shallot (echalion), finely chopped

600 g (1 lb 5 oz) fresh cuttlefish, cleaned and cut into small pieces (ask a good fishmonger)

1.2–1.5 litres (2–2½ pints) hot fresh fish stock

1 small onion, finely chopped

350 g (12 oz) paella rice, preferably Bomba rice

175 ml (6 fl oz) Txakoli or other crisp dry white wine

good pinch of saffron, soaked in 1–2 tablespoons hot water

150 g (5 oz) raw peeled prawns (shrimp)

sea salt and freshly ground black pepper

Heat a little oil in a sauté pan and gently fry the shallot until tender. Add the cuttlefish and about 200–300 ml (7–10 fl oz) of the stock to cover. Put the lid on and simmer very gently for 1 hour until really tender.

Heat a little oil in another pan and fry the onion for 10 minutes until soft. Add the rice and stir for a minute to coat in the oil. Splash in the Txakoli and cook, stirring, until it has all been absorbed.

Add the saffron and its soaking water, then gradually add the remaining stock, a ladleful at a time, stirring constantly. Allow the stock to absorb before adding the next ladleful. You want the rice to be cooked, but with some bite. This will take about 20 minutes.

Heat another frying pan with a tiny amount of oil and fry the prawns over a high heat until pink. Uncover the cuttlefish and stir it and its juices into the creamy rice along with the prawns.

Season and remove from the heat, then cover and stand for 5–10 minutes before serving.

At the table

HALIBUT A LA PLANCHA & FENNEL SALAD

136
Fish

Serves 4

5 small fennel bulbs, halved
olive oil
175 ml (6 fl oz) white wine
150 ml (5 fl oz) fresh fish stock
1 bay leaf
2 teaspoons fennel seeds
6 black peppercorns
lemon juice to taste
extra-virgin olive oil
small handful of finely chopped
    flat-leaf parsley
sea salt and freshly ground black
    pepper
4 halibut fillets (175–200 g/6–7 oz
    each)

This is my way to respect fennel, a flavour that is very close to my heart. My dad always picked wild fennel and put a sprig in his mouth, and of course I always did the same.

Here I'm using fresh and cooked fennel – they have a completely different taste and texture, which I think brings something wonderful to the halibut.

Preheat the oven to 160°C (320°F/Gas 3).

Toss four of the fennel bulbs in a little olive oil in a roasting tin. Add the wine, stock, herbs and spices. Cover with foil and roast for 50–60 minutes until really tender.

To make the fennel salad, finely slice the last fennel bulb and toss with a little lemon juice, extra-virgin olive oil and the parsley. Season and set aside.

Heat a little oil in a heavy-based frying pan, season the fish and fry, skin side down, for 4–5 minutes until almost cooked through. Turn over and fry for 30 seconds, then remove.

Spoon the roasted fennel into warmed bowls, top with the fried halibut, skin side up, and finish with some of the fennel salad.

Pintxo

BAKED CRAB

Serves 2–4

2 live brown crabs (about 750 g–
    1 kg/1 lb 10 oz–2 lb 3 oz each)
3 tablespoons olive oil
1 small onion, finely chopped
1 carrot, finely chopped
1 garlic clove, crushed
½ red chilli, finely chopped
40 g (1½ oz) plain (all-purpose) flour
175 ml (6 fl oz) full-fat (whole) milk
100 ml (3½ fl oz) fresh fish or
    vegetable stock
small handful of chopped parsley
sea salt and white pepper
3 tablespoons dry breadcrumbs

I love crab, in any way, shape or form. For me, there's nothing better than sitting with friends around a table with one of these beauties in front of you, picking all of the glorious meat out of the shell, from the claws and the legs.

For something different, pick out all of the white meat and combine with plenty of chilli, garlic parsley and olive oil and add to some spaghetti – a great quick dinner for one, and just as good served in a big bowl for everyone to dig into.

This recipe for baked crab is a little bit of work, but you can prepare it the day before, just mixing the filling the next day and adding the breadcrumbs before grilling.

Put the crabs to sleep in the freezer for 15 minutes. Bring a very large pan of water to the boil and drop in the crabs. Cover and boil for 15 minutes. Remove from the water and cool.

Twist the claws and legs off the bodies and set aside for now. Put each crab on its back. Hold the edges of the shell with your fingers and then use your thumbs to push on where the leg section joins the body and lever the body out.

Pull off the feathery dead man's fingers that are sticking out from the body. Then push with your thumbs behind the eyes, to break the section off. Remove and discard.

Scrape out all the brown meat from the sides of the shell and set aside. Use a heavy knife or hammer to crack open the claws so that you can remove all of the juicy meat. Make sure you break open the knuckles and legs to get every last bit.

Cut the leg section of the body in half and use a skewer or lobster pick to pick out all the sweet white meat from the many compartments. Clean and tidy the shells.

Heat the oil in a pan and gently fry the onion and carrot for 5 minutes to soften. Add the garlic and chilli and cook for 30 seconds, then stir in the flour. Cook for a minute, then

gradually stir in the milk and stock until you have a thick, silky béchamel sauce. Remove from the heat.

Stir all the brown and white meat and the parsley into the sauce. Season with salt and white pepper and spoon into the clean crab shells.

Heat the grill (broiler) to medium high. Scatter the crabs with breadcrumbs and grill for a couple of minutes until golden. Serve immediately.

At the table

BONITO BELLY WITH GARLIC

Serves 4

1 whole belly of bonito tuna
sea salt and freshly ground black
　　pepper
100 ml (3½ fl oz) olive oil plus extra
　　for rubbing
3 garlic cloves, sliced
1 whole dried guindilla chilli (or other
　　dried chilli)
1 tablespoon red wine vinegar
finely chopped parsley to serve

There's no such thing as getting to a fish market too early – you get the pick of the produce, and of course the exciting buzz of the catch coming in.

I arrived at Hondarribia at 5 am once, and there waiting for me was something extremely special – one of the big fishing boats had brought in 15 tonnes of bonito.

Bonito is similar to tuna but smaller, and the meat is much paler. It's so tasty though, and really sustainable too, so if you have the chance, do buy it.

If you have a local fishmonger, ask for bonito belly. If you can't get it, then mackerel is a great alternative, just ask the fishmonger to butterfly it for you.

Season the tuna belly and rub with a little oil. Heat a large heavy-based pan or chargrill pan over a high heat and sear the tuna for a couple of minutes on each side until just cooked but still a bit pink. Set aside.

Heat the oil in a pan, add the garlic and whole chilli and fry gently until just golden. Add the red wine vinegar and bubble together, then add the parsley.

Pour the garlic oil over the tuna and serve immediately with sautéed potatoes.

VEGETABLES

Vegetables are not an afterthought!

The Basque Country is a beautiful garden and the markets are just stunning. When I visit, I enjoy talking to the women and hearing about the love that they put into growing their vegetables. Walking around, chatting with them and sharing their knowledge and recipes, that really makes my day. Most of all though, I love that you can see the seasons in the markets.

As much as I love vegetables on their own, they make a great base for adding things to as well. For me, more often than not, it's cheese. Not least because as I meander around the markets, cheese is the thing that I try the most of – it's hard to resist those little tasters as you walk, and I'm always hungry.

This chapter is all about gorgeous vegetables – great, simple recipes that I want to cook over and over again. Vegetables are not an afterthought!

Pintxo

SPINACH & GOAT'S CHEESE CROQUETAS

Croquetas, croquetas, croquetas. Many people tell me that they make a beeline to Spanish restaurants for the croquetas and the tortilla, and we are very proud of ours. This is one of the most popular flavours at the restaurant; they are so creamy and moreish. You can freeze them ahead of time, and then just defrost before frying.

Makes 32–34 croquetas

500 g (1 lb 2 oz) baby leaf spinach
400 ml (13 fl oz) full-fat (whole) milk
100 ml (3½ fl oz) strong fresh
    vegetable stock
80g (3 oz) butter
125 g (4 oz) plain (all-purpose) flour
80 g (3 oz) goat's cheese, crumbled
sea salt and freshly ground black
    pepper
freshly grated nutmeg
2 large free-range eggs, beaten
125 g (4 oz) dry breadcrumbs
olive oil for deep-frying

Heat a large frying pan over a medium-high heat and add the spinach with a tiny splash of water. Cook for 3–4 minutes or until completely wilted, then run under cold water. Once cold, squeeze out all the water. Chop finely and set aside.

In a saucepan, heat the milk and the stock together. In another saucepan, melt the butter over a medium heat, add the flour and cook for 2–3 minutes. When the mixture starts to turn brown, begin adding the milk and stock very slowly until you get a really silky-smooth mix. This will take approximately 10 minutes.

Add the cheese to the mixture slowly, then add the spinach and stir constantly until it is well combined. Season with salt, pepper and a grating of nutmeg.

Spread the mixture onto a shallow tray and press a sheet of cling film (plastic wrap) over the top. Cool down in the fridge for a minimum of 2 hours.

Put some oil in the palm of your hand and roll the mixture into 30 g (1 oz) balls. If they are a little soft, pop them on a tray in the freezer to firm up for 30 minutes.

Place the beaten egg and the breadcrumbs into two separate bowls. Dip the croquetas first into the beaten egg and then into the breadcrumbs.

Heat the oil to 180°C (350°F) and fry the croquetas for around 2 minutes or until golden. Drain on paper towels, then eat straight away.

Pintxo

TOMATO SALAD WITH OLIVE OIL

Serves 2

6 beautiful tomatoes
3 tablespoons extra-virgin olive oil
sea salt

For me, there was nothing better than going to my dad's vegetable garden, which is now my brother's, on a hot summer's day to pick tomatoes straight from the plants. The smell of the tomatoes would always hit me first, then we would wash them in pure spring water and eat them. That's what I call a perfect start to the day.

This is another great recipe where the two main ingredients make a perfect simple pintxo or side dish for grilled fish or meat. Tomatoes and olive oil are two of my favourite ingredients. I always go to the restaurant Bodegón Donostiarra for their tomato salad. I like to use Manzanilla Cacereña olive oil in this recipe, but any that you have will work just as well.

If you want you can peel the tomatoes first – this will give a different, softer texture. Simply bring a pan of water to the boil and have a bowl of cold water to one side. Make a small, very shallow cross in the base of the tomatoes with a sharp knife, then drop them into the boiling water for 5–10 seconds. Scoop out with a slotted spoon and put in the cold water. The skins will start to curl away from the flesh, making them easy to peel off.

Cut the tomatoes into roughly 2 cm (¾ in) pieces. Place in a bowl, keeping all the juices.

Add the olive oil and salt. The salad is now ready to enjoy – it's as easy as that!

Pintxo

PAN-FRIED GUINDILLAS

Serves 4

250 g (9 oz) fresh guindillas
3 tablespoons olive oil
sea salt

Guindilla is a chilli pepper traditionally grown in the Basque area. They have a lovely, mild flavour. This type of guindilla grows in the area of Ibarra in Gipuzcoa and they can grow as long as 5–12 cm (2–4½ in). Harvested at the end of July, they have a beautiful green-yellow colour, but almost no heat. The most popular way that you'll find the guindillas is in a jar preserved with wine vinegar, and they are used as a garnish in many different dishes. I particularly love to add them to pulses.

Nowadays, it's also very popular to simply fry these lovely things, when the season comes around, just as you would with Padrón peppers.

Heat the oil in a frying pan. When the oil is hot, add the guindillas and sauté well for about 5–6 minutes.

Continue until you see the skins are separating from the flesh, then take the chillies out, sprinkle with sea salt and enjoy with a nice cold beer.

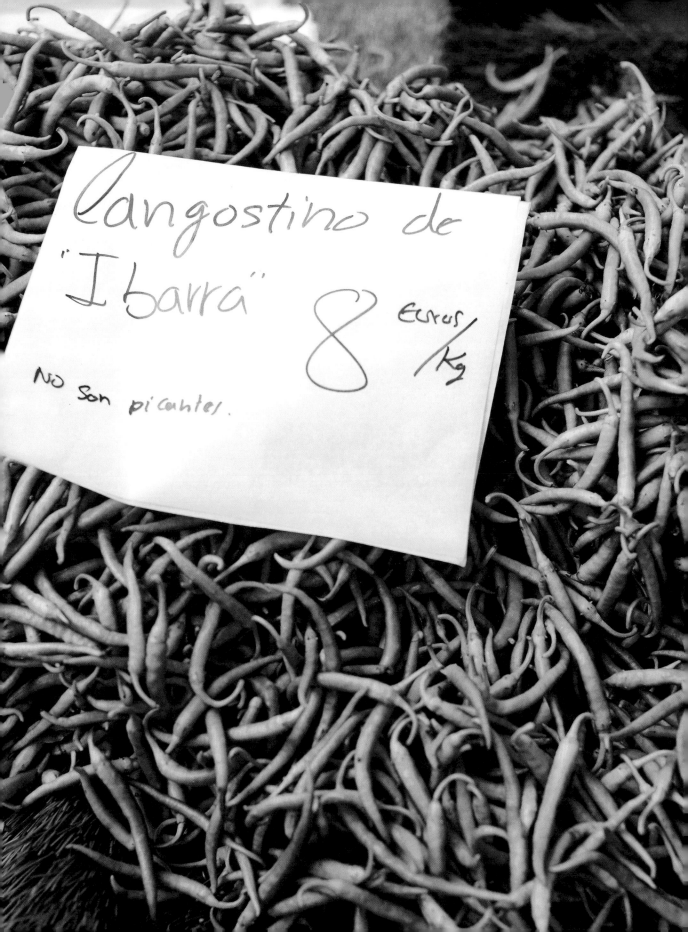

Pintxo

PAN-FRIED CEPS WITH EGG YOLK

Serves 4

olive oil
200 g (7 oz) fresh ceps (porcini),
  cleaned and finely sliced
sea salt and freshly ground black
  pepper
4 super-fresh free-range egg yolks
finely chopped parsley to serve

You would never think this mix would work, but it is just incredible. Finding good mushrooms is very important, but using a proper fresh, high-quality egg is the key in this combination. I always make this recipe when I get my first British ceps, but you could use other mild mushrooms if you can't get hold of ceps.

In a large frying pan, heat a good layer of oil over a medium heat. When it is hot, add the mushrooms and fry for a couple of minutes, then turn over and do the same again. Season with plenty of salt and black pepper.

Divide the mushrooms among four warmed plates, add an egg yolk to the centre of each, and scatter with parsley. Once served, immediately mix all together and eat!

Pintxo

CLASSIC TORTILLA

Serves 2

200 ml (7 fl oz) olive oil for the potato
3 medium (about 375 g/13 oz)
      potatoes, finely sliced
1 small onion, finely sliced
4 large free-range eggs
3 tablespoons olive oil for the tortilla
sea salt and freshly ground black
      pepper

This is a bit quicker then the traditional tortilla, as you caramelise the onions first. It also makes omelettes that are a little smaller than normal, so perfect if you're just cooking for one or want to use as a side dish to something else.

I think that the Tomato Salad with Olive Oil on page 153 is the perfect marriage to this tortilla.

In a saucepan, heat the oil over a medium heat. Add the potatoes and the onion and cook for around 10 minutes or until they are soft. Drain the oil. While the mixture is still warm, divide in half.

In a bowl, beat two of the eggs and add half of the potato and onion mixture, combining well.

Heat half of the oil in a non-stick 15 cm (6 in) frying pan. When the oil is hot, add the mixture. Swirl the pan over a high heat until the mixture starts to set around the edges, then reduce the heat and cook for 4–5 minutes until it just starts to set and the bottom and sides are golden, but it is still quite loose in the middle.

Cover the pan with a flat lid or board and turn the tortilla carefully onto it. Don't worry that it is still quite runny –it will all come back together when you continue to cook it. Slide the tortilla back into the pan, then put the pan back on a low heat. Use a spatula to tuck the edges of the tortilla under to give it its characteristic curved look. Cook for a couple of minutes, then turn onto a board and keep warm. Make the second tortilla using the remaining ingredients.

The tortillas should still be lovely and juicy in the middle when you cut into them.

Pintxo

TOASTS WITH REQUESÓN, RED PEPPERS & THYME

Makes 20 pintxos

3 giant Spanish or 5 large red (bell)
   peppers
handful of thyme, leaves stripped
2 tablespoons small capers, rinsed
   and squeezed dry
extra-virgin olive oil
sea salt and freshly ground black
   pepper
20 slices of baguette

for the requesón
1 litre (34 fl oz) full-fat (whole) milk
3 cloves
10 black peppercorns
pinch of sea salt
juice of 1–2 lemons

Requesón is a type of simple curd cheese. I always make double quantities, as I love it. It's so versatile that I have it for breakfast, on toast with some honey. The best thing is that it also keeps in the fridge for up to 5 days as well.

As a pintxo, it's the perfect accompaniment to beer, but also use it in a salad or as a great garnish to go with grilled fish.

To make the cheese, heat the milk with the cloves, peppercorns and a pinch of salt until it reaches 85°C (185°F). Remove from the heat and add the juice of 1 lemon and stir. Stand for 10 minutes until the curds have separated from the whey. If you need to, you can add a little more lemon juice, a tablespoon at a time.

Line a colander with muslin, stand over a bowl and strain the milk through. Leave to stand for 30 minutes, very gently squeezing to remove most of the liquid from the cheese. Leave to cool, then scoop the solid curds from the colander into a container, removing as many of the peppercorns and cloves as you can see, and leave to chill in the fridge.

Using a blowtorch or under a very hot grill (broiler), blacken the pepper skins all over. Put into a freezer bag, seal and stand for 5 minutes to steam. Remove the skins from the peppers. Halve and discard the seeds, then finely slice, saving the juices.

Toss the peppers and juices with the thyme leaves, capers and a good glug of olive oil. Season to taste.

Toast the baguette slices. Top with the peppers and then crumble over a little of the requesón cheese. Drizzle with extra olive oil and serve.

Pintxo

CHERRY & ALMOND SOUP

Serves 4

500 g (1 lb 2 oz) cherries
1 small cucumber, peeled and cut
    into small cubes
1 tomato, cut into small cubes
1 garlic clove, sliced
1 small onion, cut into small cubes
50 ml (2 fl oz) extra-virgin olive oil,
    plus a splash
30–40 ml (1–1½ fl oz) sherry vinegar
sea salt and freshly ground black
    pepper
15 g (½ oz) toasted flaked almonds

Walking around La Brecha market in San Sebastián, I fell in love with a stall where the old farmer lady had the most amazing cherries, sitting next to the onions and tomatoes. They looked so perfect together that I started thinking about how I could combine all of these stunning ingredients into a dish. This is what I came up with, and I think it's a perfect soup for summertime. Thanks Señora; I will share this recipe with you next time I'm visiting.

Stone the cherries, cut in half and reserve 100 g (3½ oz).

Combine the remaining cherries with the cucumber, tomato, garlic, onion and olive oil. Cover and keep in the fridge for 3 hours. After this time, place in a food processor, add 30 ml (1 fl oz) of the vinegar, salt and pepper and blend until smooth. Add extra vinegar to taste.

Serve in small bowls garnished with the reserved cherries, the almonds and a splash of olive oil.

Pintxo

WHITE ASPARAGUS WITH OLIVE OIL MAYONNAISE

Serves 4

16 white asparagus

for the mayonnaise
2 free-range egg yolks
1 teaspoon white wine vinegar
sea salt and freshly ground black
    pepper
150 ml (5 fl oz) olive oil
lemon juice to taste

My mum always has a few jars of white asparagus in the house, not least because it's something that my dad and I used to have for dinner when I was little. I love to have these with some mayonnaise as in this recipe. I'd never tried the fresh ones until I moved to Madrid, and now I definitely prefer this way of serving them, but sometimes I do hanker for the ones in the jar when I visit my mum, and those childhood memories come flooding back.

First, prepare the mayonnaise. In a mixing bowl, whisk together the egg yolks, vinegar and a pinch of salt and pepper, then very slowly add the olive oil, whisking vigorously, until you get a thick and smooth mayonnaise. Check the seasoning and add lemon juice to taste

Clean the asparagus well, then cut the bottoms off and peel with a potato peeler.

In a large saucepan, bring plenty of water to the boil. When it is boiling, add some salt, followed by the asparagus. Boil them over a medium heat for 5–8 minutes, depending on how thick the asparagus are, until they are lovely and tender.

Divide the asparagus among four warmed plates and serve with the mayonnaise and some black pepper.

Pintxo

AUBERGINE, HONEY & BLUE CHEESE OMELETTE

Serves 4

500 ml (17 fl oz) olive oil
300 g (10½ oz) aubergines
    (eggplant), sliced
200 g (7 oz) waxy potatoes, sliced
8 free-range eggs
sea salt and freshly ground black
    pepper
75 g (2½ oz) blue cheese
2–4 tablespoons honey

This is proof of how versatile an omelette can be. We cooked this at my little tapas bar José, and now everyone asks us when it's coming back.

Serve hot or cold, it really doesn't matter. It's delicious.

Heat the oil in large pan and very gently fry the aubergine and potatoes for 25–30 minutes until the potatoes are tender. Drain well (reserve the oil to use later). Break up the potatoes into smaller pieces with a spoon.

Beat the eggs with plenty of seasoning in a large bowl. Add the cheese and honey to the vegetables and mix well. Add all of the ingredients to the bowl of beaten egg and gently mix.

Heat 3 tablespoons of the reserved oil in a 23 cm (9 in) non-stick frying pan. When the oil is hot, pour in the omelette mixture. Swirl the pan over a high heat until the mixture starts to set around the edges, then reduce the heat and cook for 4–5 minutes until it just starts to set and the bottom and sides are golden, but it is still quite loose in the middle.

Cover the pan with a flat lid or board and turn the tortilla carefully onto it. Don't worry that it is still quite runny – it will all come back together when you continue to cook it. Slide the tortilla back into the pan, then put the pan back on a low heat. Use a spatula to tuck the edges of the tortilla under to give it its characteristic curved look. Cook for a couple of minutes, then turn onto a board and serve. It should still be lovely and juicy in the middle when you cut into it.

Pintxo

SLOW-COOKED BROAD BEANS WITH POACHED EGG

Serves 6 as a starter

3 kg (6½ lb) broad beans
100 ml (3½ fl oz) olive oil
3 medium French shallots, finely
    chopped
150 ml (5 fl oz) dry white wine
750 ml (25 fl oz) fresh vegetable
    stock
6 free-range eggs
150 g (5 oz) pecorino, Roncal or
    Idiazábal cheese, shaved
small handful of finely chopped
    flat-leaf parsley
freshly ground black pepper
extra-virgin olive oil to drizzle

In Spain we love to cook broad beans for a long time until they become really soft and nutty. This is my interpretation of a very tasty recipe that is popular in the Basque Country, but my mum in Extremadura also loves to cook it when we get the first broad beans. Here we are using only the beans, but at home my family picked the broad beans so young that you could use the whole thing, cutting them very finely. Buy the broad beans as young as you can because then you will not need to double pod the beans; or use frozen beans and keep the recipe up your sleeve for last-minute dinner parties. You can serve this as a starter or as a side dish for grilled fish or meat.

Pod the broad beans.

In a saucepan, heat the oil over a medium heat, add the shallots and cook for 10 minutes until lightly golden and soft. Add the broad beans and mix together well, cooking for another 5 minutes, then add the wine, bubbling for a minute or two to reduce the alcohol. Add two-thirds of the stock, cover and cook for a further 30 minutes, adding more stock if the broad beans start to get too dry.

Meanwhile, poach the eggs in a medium saucepan of salted simmering water for 3 minutes or until just cooked and ready to serve.

Spoon the beans into six warmed bowls, top with a poached egg and scatter with the cheese, parsley, black pepper and a drizzle of extra-virgin olive oil.

Pintxo

WARM BRAISED ARTICHOKES & TOMATOES

Serves 6

olive oil
2 French shallots, finely sliced
2 carrots, finely chopped
3 garlic cloves, finely sliced
600 g (1 lb 5 oz) good quality
    tomatoes, chopped
150–175 ml (5–6 fl oz) dry white wine
1 tablespoon white wine vinegar
sea salt and freshly ground black
    pepper
750 ml (25 fl oz) fresh vegetable
    stock
6 globe artichokes
extra-virgin olive oil to drizzle

I love to cook the artichokes with plenty of vegetables such as tomatoes, onions and carrots with some garlic, a little white wine and a splash of vinegar. I think this works much better than cooking the artichokes in water and adding lemon or vinegar.

Heat a good amount of oil in a large saucepan. Gently fry the shallots and carrots for 10 minutes. Add the garlic, then add the tomatoes and white wine.

Bubble for a few minutes, then add the vinegars and plenty of seasoning. Add the stock and bring to the boil. Reduce to a simmer, cover and cook for 15–20 minutes.

Meanwhile, prepare the artichokes. Trim off the stems and remove the very thick leaves from the base. Trim any spines from the top of the leaves. Add to the pan, base side down, cover and cook for 20–40 minutes, depending on size. Check to see if the artichokes are done – a leaf should pull away easily from the globe. If not, cook for a further 10 minutes and test again.

Serve the artichokes with the tomato broth, chunks of fresh bread and lots of extra-virgin olive oil to drizzle. Once you have pulled off and nibbled the larger leaves, throw away the rest of the smaller leaves and scrape away the choke to reveal the heart.

Pintxo

GRILLED GREEN & WHITE ASPARAGUS WITH IDIAZÁBAL SMOKED CHEESE

Serves 4

12 white asparagus
12 green asparagus
3 tablespoons olive oil
100 g (3½ oz) Idiazábal smoked cheese, sliced
extra-virgin olive oil
sea salt and freshly ground black pepper

We're so lucky in Britain with the amazing array of produce that we can find on our doorsteps – British asparagus is one of my favourites and the season never comes soon enough for me. I always feel inspired when I first see asparagus on the shelves, but nothing frustrates me more than to see asparagus on the menu or on the shelves in winter. It doesn't make sense!

I love to combine the best British produce with classic Spanish ingredients, and this cheese from the Basque Country complements the asparagus perfectly.

Blanch the white asparagus in a pan of boiling salted water for 3–4 minutes, then drain. Put both the white and green asparagus in a large dish with the oil and mix together well.

Heat a chargrill pan over a high heat. Turn the heat down to medium, place half of the asparagus on the pan and grill them for a couple of minutes, then turn over.

When the asparagus are ready, keep ithem in a warm place and cook the rest.

Divide the asparagus among four warmed plates and add the cheese, drizzling over some more olive oil and seasoning with sea salt and fresh black pepper.

Pintxo

ROASTED ONIONS STUFFED WITH PARSLEY & GARLIC MIGAS

Serves 4

8 small onions
olive oil
2 garlic cloves, finely chopped
50 g (2 oz) stale bread, cut into small cubes
25 g (1 oz) dried apricots, chopped
50 g (2 oz) toasted pine nuts
sea salt and freshly ground black pepper
small handful of chopped parsley

Onions never feature very often on menus or in books as a dish in their own right, which is a great shame as they are so versatile. I like to stuff onions with fried beef or lamb mince, or cheese and walnuts, and then roast them. This particular recipe is really good to make as a pintxo, and it's something that people probably wouldn't expect, so you will impress them.

Migas are small fried breadcrumbs that you add to dishes for some texture, normally made with plenty of olive oil, garlic and peppers.

I have such great memories of chatting with my grandfather when he was cutting the leftover bread into small pieces in order to make the migas. My mum would then make them the following morning – gorgeous little golden nuggets!

Cut the base and top off the onions, blanch them for 20 minutes in simmering water to soften them, then peel off the skins. Use a small knife to remove the heart of each of the onions and finely chop.

Preheat the oven to 170°C (340°F/Gas 3).

Heat a little oil in a pan and fry the chopped onion hearts with the garlic for a few minutes. Add the bread, apricots and toasted pine nuts and fry together for a few minutes. Season and add the parsley.

Stuff the mixture into the onions and place on a baking tray. Drizzle with oil and roast for 20–25 minutes until the onions are tender and golden. Scatter with sea salt and serve.

SPINACH, BLUE CHEESE & PINE NUT EMPANADAS

Serves 6

olive oil
1.2 kg (2 lb 10 oz) spinach
200 g (7 oz) soft blue cheese,
   crumbled
100 g (3½ oz) toasted pine nuts
sea salt and freshly ground black
   pepper
good grating of fresh nutmeg
1 free-range egg, beaten to glaze

for the pastry
500 g (1 lb 2 oz) plain (all-purpose)
   flour, plus extra to dust
1 teaspoon fine sea salt
200 g (7 oz) cold unsalted butter,
   cut into cubes
1 free-range egg
75 ml (2½ fl oz) cold water
2 teaspoons white wine vinegar
1 free-range egg yolk, beaten

I use urdiña cheese for this recipe. It's a blue cheese made with raw sheep's milk – big and strong flavours, my favourite. If it's tricky to find, buy a strong Stilton. I love English cheese too, so this works really well as an alternative.

Make the pastry first. Tip the flour and salt into a bowl and rub the butter in with your fingertips until it looks like breadcrumbs. Mix the egg with the cold water and vinegar, add to the bowl and mix in quickly with a flat knife. Bring together with your hands and knead briefly until smooth, then shape into a disc, wrap in cling film (plastic wrap) and chill for at least 30 minutes.

Heat a little oil in a very large pan and sauté the spinach until it is really wilted (you may need to do this in batches). Place in a colander and squeeze out as much liquid as you can, then finely chop and tip into a bowl.

Add the cheese and pine nuts to the warm spinach and season with salt, pepper and lots of fresh nutmeg. Allow to cool.

Preheat the oven to 200°C (400°F/Gas 6).

Divide the dough into 6 even pieces and place under a damp tea towel (dish towel) to stop them drying out. One at a time, roll them out on a lightly floured surface until they are 16–18 cm (6–7 in) in diameter. Place a sixth of the mixture into the centre of one half of the circle. Brush the edge with beaten egg yolk, then fold over and crimp with your fingers.

Place on a lined baking sheet and repeat with the rest of the dough and filling.

Brush the empanadas all over with the beaten egg and bake for 25–30 minutes until golden. Cool a little before serving.

At the table

PORRUSALDA

Serves 4–6

2 tablespoons olive oil
1 onion, finely sliced
750 ml (25 fl oz) strong fresh
    vegetable stock
3 carrots, thickly sliced
3 leeks, cut into pieces
4 medium potatoes, cut into 1.5 cm
    (¾ in) cubes
sea salt

This is a popular dish from the Navarra and Rioja regions, which I always have to eat when I visit San Sebastián. The name comes from the word '*puerro*' ('leek' in Spanish). It is a very simple recipe in which it is important to use a good stock. In this case, I have used a very nice and strong vegetable stock, but you could also use chicken stock.

If you feel like something slightly different, you can also add chorizo to make a *porrusalda riojana*.

In a saucepan, heat the oil and add the onion, cooking it through but without letting it change colour.

Add the stock and bring to the boil, then add the carrots, leeks and potatoes and cook for 15–20 minutes or until the vegetables are tender. Season with sea salt and serve hot with some crusty bread.

At the table

ALUBIAS DE TOLOSA

Serves 4–6

500 g (1 lb 2 oz) alubias de Tolosa
    or turtle beans
1 small onion, finely chopped
5 tablespoons olive oil
sea salt

These beans can be served as a starter or together with some vegetables, pork or cabbage. For me, just a plate of them with some *guindillas de Ibarra* in vinegar makes me very happy. This recipe is the traditional one and was given to me by a farmer in Ordiza market. He was very clear about telling me that the beans must be cooked slowly over a very low heat!

Normally in Tolosa they don't soak the beans in water the day before. The sauce from these beans is really rich and thick and it will be even thicker if you cook the beans the day before.

Put all of the ingredients in a large saucepan with 1.5 litres (2½ pints) of water (but don't add any salt at this stage).

Bring slowly to the boil and cook for 10 minutes, then reduce the heat right down and cook very gently for 2 hours. When the beans are almost ready, add some salt and keep cooking slowly until they are tender but still holding their shape and the sauce is really thick.

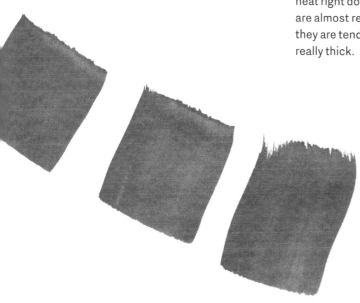

At the table

WARM SALAD OF BABY ARTICHOKES & BROAD BEANS WITH WALNUTS & MINT

Serves 4

olive oil
2 French shallots, finely sliced
2 garlic cloves, finely sliced
zest of 1 lemon
10–12 baby artichokes, halved
500 ml (17 fl oz) fresh vegetable
    stock
sea salt and freshly ground black
    pepper
300 g (10½ oz) freshly podded
    broad beans, from about 1.2 kg
    (2 lb 10 oz) broad bean pods
50 ml (2 fl oz) double (heavy) cream
100 g (3½ oz) walnut halves
handful of mint
extra-virgin olive oil to drizzle

We love artichokes in Spain, from the ones in the jar to the very overcooked – yes, really.

I do like good quality preserved food in tins and jars, but the artichokes are my favourite. This is a great supper dish, one that you will cook again and again.

Heat a little oil in a sauté pan and gently fry the shallots until soft. Add the garlic and lemon zest, then add the artichoke halves and the stock. Season and bring to a simmer, then cover and cook for 30–35 minutes.

Add the broad beans and cook for a further 10 minutes. Stir in the cream and check the seasoning.

Toast the walnuts in a pan until lightly golden, then tip onto a baking sheet lined with non-stick silicone or baking paper to cool.

Spoon the warm artichokes and beans into four bowls with their lovely juices. Scatter with the walnuts and mint and drizzle with extra-virgin olive oil to serve.

LENTILS & GOAT'S CHEESE WITH CARAMELISED WALNUTS

Serves 4

olive oil
1 onion, finely chopped
1 carrot, finely chopped
1 celery stalk, finely chopped
1 garlic clove, crushed
1 bay leaf
few sprigs of oregano
300 g (10½ oz) Spanish pardina lentils
600 ml (20 fl oz) fresh vegetable stock
2 ripe vine tomatoes, skins removed and chopped
75 g (2½ oz) caster (superfine) sugar
handful of walnuts
100 g (3½ oz) soft goat's cheese

It's not very often you meet a young person such as Kepa, an enthusiastic chap in his early twenties, who is already producing the most amazing goat's cheese. I met him at his farm in Amorebieta-Etxano, where the views were something to behold.

This is a really nice, simple salad I made using Kepa's fantastic cheese with plenty of carrots, onions, celery, garlic and some tomatoes. The caramelised walnuts are great as an aperitif with your beer – just add some flakes of salt and they are ready.

Heat a little oil in a deep pan and gently fry the onion, carrot and celery for 15 minutes until really tender. Add the garlic and fry for a minute more, then add the bay leaf, oregano and lentils. Pour in the stock and add the tomatoes. Bring to the boil, then cover and simmer for 30–35 minutes until the lentils are starting to break down and make a lovely thick sauce.

Meanwhile, put the sugar in a pan with 2 tablespoons of water and dissolve over a low heat. Bring to the boil and cook for 4–5 minutes until you have a golden caramel, then add the walnuts and mix together to coat.

Tip the walnuts onto a baking sheet lined with greased baking paper and leave to cool.

Spoon the lentils into four warmed bowls, add a scoop of goat's cheese to each bowl, then top with the caramelised walnuts.

At the table

WILD MUSHROOMS & TRUFFLE WITH DUCK EGG ON TOAST

Serves 4

olive oil
2 garlic cloves, finely sliced
500 g (1 lb 2 oz) wild mushrooms,
    cleaned
sea salt and freshly ground black
    pepper
4 duck eggs
4 thick slices of sourdough
1 whole garlic clove
extra-virgin olive oil to drizzle
fresh black truffle shavings

This is what I call a satisfying breakfast!

To make this properly, you must keep the egg in a sealed container with the truffle for at least a week. The egg will take on the aroma of the truffle, giving it a wonderful flavour. Proper earthy food. The aroma comes back to me often – I just love it.

Heat a good glug of olive oil in a pan and gently fry the sliced garlic for a minute, then increase the heat, add the mushrooms and fry for about 5 minutes until they are tender and all the moisture has been absorbed. Season with sea salt and plenty of freshly ground black pepper.

Meanwhile, heat some more oil in another frying pan over a high heat and fry the duck eggs so that the edges of the whites become really crispy.

Toast the bread, rub with a little of the whole garlic and drizzle with extra-virgin olive oil.

Pile the mushrooms onto the toasts, top each with a fried egg and finish with some shavings of fresh black truffle and a drizzle more of extra-virgin olive oil.

At the table

SWISS CHARD STEW WITH PIMENTÓN

Serves 4

olive oil
1 large onion, finely chopped
2 garlic cloves, finely sliced
1 red pepper, deseeded and finely
    sliced
1 teaspoon pimentón
500 g (1 lb 2 oz) floury potatoes,
    sliced
750 g (1 lb 10 oz) Swiss chard, stalks
    roughly chopped and leaves
    shredded
750 ml (25 fl oz) fresh vegetable
    stock
sea salt and freshly ground black
    pepper

I'd never cooked with Swiss or rainbow chard until I started working at Eyre Brothers in London. I fell in love with the beautiful colours – just looking at it makes me happy.

This stew is an interpretation of my mum's recipe because even though we overcook the chard very slightly, my mum cooks it even for longer!

I normally serve this as a starter, but you can also use this recipe as a side for some grilled fish or chicken.

Heat a little oil in a casserole dish and gently fry the onion for 10 minutes until softened. Add the garlic and fry for a minute, then add the red pepper and pimentón and fry for a few more minutes.

Add the potatoes, Swiss chard stalks and stock, season well and bring to a simmer. Cover and cook for 20 minutes, adding the leaves for the last few minutes, until you have a lovely thick stew. Serve with lots of crusty bread to mop up the juices.

At the table

ROASTED PUMPKIN & RONCAL WITH WALNUT VINAIGRETTE

Serves 4

1.5 kg (3 lb 5 oz) pumpkin or squash,
   peeled, deseeded and cut into
   wedges
olive oil
few sprigs of rosemary
1 bulb garlic, cloves separated
80 g (3 oz) walnut halves
75 g (2½ oz) Roncal cheese, shaved

for the dressing
2 tablespoons cider vinegar
little drizzle of honey
sea salt and freshly ground black
   pepper
3 tablespoons extra-virgin olive oil
1 tablespoon walnut oil

In my mind, this is a perfect salad, not pretentious in any way – just amazing ingredients put together to create a great supper dish or light lunch.

Roncal is a hard, creamy sheep milk cheese that is made in the Valle of Roncal in one of seven villages around the Basque region. If you can't find it, substitute with semi-cured manchego.

Preheat the oven to 200°C (400°F/Gas 6).

Toss the pumpkin with plenty of oil in a roasting tin and add the rosemary and garlic. Roast for 30–40 minutes until tender.

Put a baking tray with the walnuts into the oven for the last 7–10 minutes of the cooking time to roast until lightly golden. Set the pumpkin and walnuts aside to cool a little.

To make the dressing, whisk the vinegar with the honey and some salt and pepper. Whisk in the oils until emulsified.

On a serving platter, toss the roasted pumpkin and garlic with the cheese and walnuts. Pour over the dressing, mix together and serve with fresh bread.

DESSERTS

I love Basque desserts!

Basque people have really lovely traditional dessert recipes, based on using local nuts, honey and corn. These recipes have stayed around for a long time because they use up the surplus from the harvests, so it always makes sense to cook them.

You might find that you recognise some of these as French desserts, and this is simply because of the geography of the Basque Country. It is a close neighbour to France, so naturally ideas have made their way across the borders over the years. I love Basque desserts because they are not very sweet!

CUAJADA WITH HONEY & WALNUTS

Serves 4–6

1 litre (34 fl oz) raw milk
25 g (1 oz) rennet
honey to drizzle
roughly chopped walnuts to serve

Cuajada is like Marmite – you either love it or you hate it! Well, I love both!

Cuajada, or as it's called in the Basque Country, *mamia*, is a type of cheese that is very popular in the north of Spain. Traditionally, it was made with sheep's milk but is now normally made with raw cow's milk. Like fromage frais, it's a smooth cheese with a really creamy and delicate texture.

You can serve it on its own with some fresh walnuts and honey as I have here; I really enjoy it for breakfast. The recipe works with raw milk, which is not difficult to find these days – either online or perhaps at your local market.

Bring the milk to the boil. Pour into a jug and leave to cool until it reaches 37°C (99°F) on a digital thermometer, then sprinkle the rennet evenly over the top. Stir gently to dissolve, then pour into four or six individual pots and leave to set and chill for about 4 hours without stirring.

Once set, drizzle with honey, scatter with walnuts and serve.

APPLE TATIN WITH SALTED HONEY ICE CREAM

Serves 6

200 g (7 oz) caster (superfine) sugar
50 g (2 oz) unsalted butter
few sprigs of lemon thyme
5–6 dessert apples, peeled, cored
    and halved
500 g (1 lb 2 oz) all-butter puff pastry
plain (all-purpose) flour to dust

for the ice cream
600 ml (20 fl oz) full-fat (whole) milk
50 g (2 oz) caster (superfine) sugar
190 g (6½ oz) runny honey
6 free-range egg yolks
1 teaspoon flaky sea salt
500 ml (17 fl oz) double (heavy)
    cream

Tip: *If you don't have an ice-cream maker, pour the mixture into a deep plastic container and freeze for 2 hours, then beat with an electric hand whisk to break up the crystals and freeze for a further hour. Repeat twice, then freeze until solid.*

You may ask why a famous French dessert is in a book about Basque cuisine. Well, there are two main reasons for this. Firstly, the Basque region has an abundance of delicious apples and secondly, I just love this recipe. What more can I say?

To make the ice cream, heat the milk with the sugar until almost boiling. Beat the honey, egg yolks and salt together in a bowl until light and fluffy. Pour the hot milk over the egg mixture, stirring until smooth.

Pour the mixture back into a clean pan and put over a medium-low heat and cook, stirring constantly, until you have a thick, smooth custard. Pour into a bowl and, when cold, stir in the cream. Pour into an ice-cream maker and churn until set, then scoop into a container and freeze until ready to serve.

For the tatin, pour the sugar into a heavy-based ovenproof frying pan with a 20 cm (8 in) diameter base and add a couple of tablespoons of water. Stir to mix, then place over a low heat and cook very gently, stirring, until the sugar has dissolved.

Stop stirring, increase the heat to high and bubble until you have a dark golden caramel. Add the butter, stirring quickly until smooth, then put the apples, cut side up, into the pan, with the thyme. Return to a low heat and cook for 10 minutes, then set aside to cool completely.

Preheat the oven to 200°C (400°F/Gas 6).

Roll the pastry out on a lightly floured surface and cut a round a bit bigger than the pan. Tuck the pastry over the top of the apples so it sits snuggly round the side of the pan.

Bake for 25–30 minutes until the pastry is golden. Leave to stand for 10 minutes before turning out onto a plate and serving with the salted honey ice cream.

PANTXINETA

Serves 8

350 ml (12 fl oz) full-fat (whole) milk
1 vanilla pod, split and seeds
    scraped
5 free-range egg yolks
75 g (2½ oz) caster (superfine) sugar
40 g (1½ oz) plain (all-purpose) flour,
    plus extra to dust
1 tablespoon cornflour (cornstarch)
25 g (1 oz) ground almonds
½ teaspoon almond extract
500 g (1 lb 2 oz) all-butter puff pastry
1 whole free-range egg, beaten
25 g (1 oz) flaked almonds
icing (confectioners') sugar to dust

In the beginning of the 20th century, San Sebastián was the place where Spanish royalty and the aristocracy would go to spend the Summer. It was during these times that the restaurants and patisseries were imitating the cuisine from France, and the *pantxineta* was the evolution of the classic French tart. A baker called Oteagui first started making it this way. Pantxineta is a tart of puff-pastry and custard in the main, but I have added some ground almonds to give it a slightly different dimension in both flavour and texture.

Heat the milk with the vanilla seeds and pod until just boiling. Beat the egg yolks with the caster sugar, then beat in the flours until you have a smooth paste.

Sieve over the hot milk and mix together, then pour back into the pan and cook over a medium heat until you have a smooth, very thick custard. Spoon into a bowl and cool a little, then add the ground almonds and almond extract, cover with cling film (plastic wrap) and leave to cool completely.

Preheat the oven to 200°C (350°F/Gas 6). Halve the pastry and roll out on a lightly floured surface until you can cut a circle about 28 cm (11 in) in diameter. Place on a baking sheet lined with baking paper. Spread the cream filling out over the base, leaving a 2–3 cm (1 in) border all around.

Roll out the other half of the pastry to cut a 30 cm (12 in) diameter circle. Brush the exposed edge of the bottom half with beaten egg, then gently lay the second pastry round over the top and press with a fork to seal the edges.

Brush the top of the pastry all over with the beaten egg, make a few small holes with the tip of a small sharp knife to allow steam to escape and scatter with the flaked almonds. Chill for 15 minutes, then bake for 30–35 minutes until golden and puffed up. Allow to cool before sprinkling with icing sugar and serving.

ALMOND & CHERRY CAKE

Serves 8–10

4 free-range egg yolks
175 g (6 oz) caster (superfine) sugar
150 g (5 oz) ground almonds
zest of 2 lemons
2 free-range egg whites
150 g (5 oz) fresh cherries, pitted
flaked almonds to scatter

I met a really lovely lady called Agustina at the Ordizia market in May, where she offered me her first cherries of the season. She was so proud of them and it's wonderful to see people like her get so excited about their produce. And rightly so. She told me how to eat them and suggested that if I liked to bake, then making a cake with almonds would complement the cherries perfectly.

And here it is ... this is in your honour, Señora Agustina!

Preheat the oven to 170°C (340°F/Gas 3) and grease and line a 23 cm (9 in) loose-bottomed cake tin.

Beat the egg yolks with the caster sugar until really light and fluffy. Add the ground almonds and lemon zest. In a clean bowl, beat the egg whites until just holding their shape, then carefully fold them into the cake mix.

Spoon the mixture into the cake tin and scatter over the pitted cherries. Sprinkle with almonds and bake for 25 minutes until lightly golden and a skewer inserted into the centre comes out clean. Leave to cool in the tin for a few minutes, then turn out onto a wire rack to cool completely. Serve warm or cold.

CHOCOLATE POTS WITH TEJAS DE TOLOSA

Serves 6

200 g (7 oz) dark chocolate, broken
    into pieces
75 ml (2½ fl oz) full-fat (whole) milk,
    warmed to blood temperature
200 ml (7 fl oz) double (heavy) cream,
    out of the fridge for 20 minutes

for the tejas de Tolosa biscuits
1 free-range egg white
50 g (2 oz) caster (superfine) sugar
1 tablespoon plain (all-purpose) flour
few drops of vanilla extract
25 g (1 oz) unsalted butter, melted
    and cooled
flaked almonds to sprinkle (optional)

The *tejas* and *cigarrilos de Tolosa* have a long history and were created in Tolosa for the very famous pastry shop, Eceiza, which opened in 1924. They were originally intended as a dessert, but you'll now find that they are typically served with coffee instead, both in restaurants and in the cider houses.

This is my way of making them … they are dangerous, as once you start eating them, you won't be able to stop dipping them in the chocolate. Try adding some drops of really good extra-virgin olive oil and few flakes of salt to the chocolate pot too. You won't regret it.

Preheat the oven to 190°C (375°F/Gas 5). Line two baking sheets with baking paper.

To make the biscuits, beat the egg white and caster sugar with a fork until frothy. Sift over the flour and fold in. Add the vanilla extract, then lastly add the cooled melted butter.

Spoon the mixture onto the baking sheets in dollops about 8 cm (3 in) wide. Sprinkle with the flaked almonds, if using, and bake for 6–8 minutes until lightly golden. Have a rolling pin ready and, as soon as the biscuits are out of the oven, lay them over the rolling pin so that they cool and harden in a curled shape. Set aside on a wire rack.

Melt the chocolate in a bain-marie until smooth. Very slowly add the milk, then the cream. Pour into six small pots or glasses and leave to set in a cool place (or in the fridge if your kitchen is very hot) before serving with the biscuits.

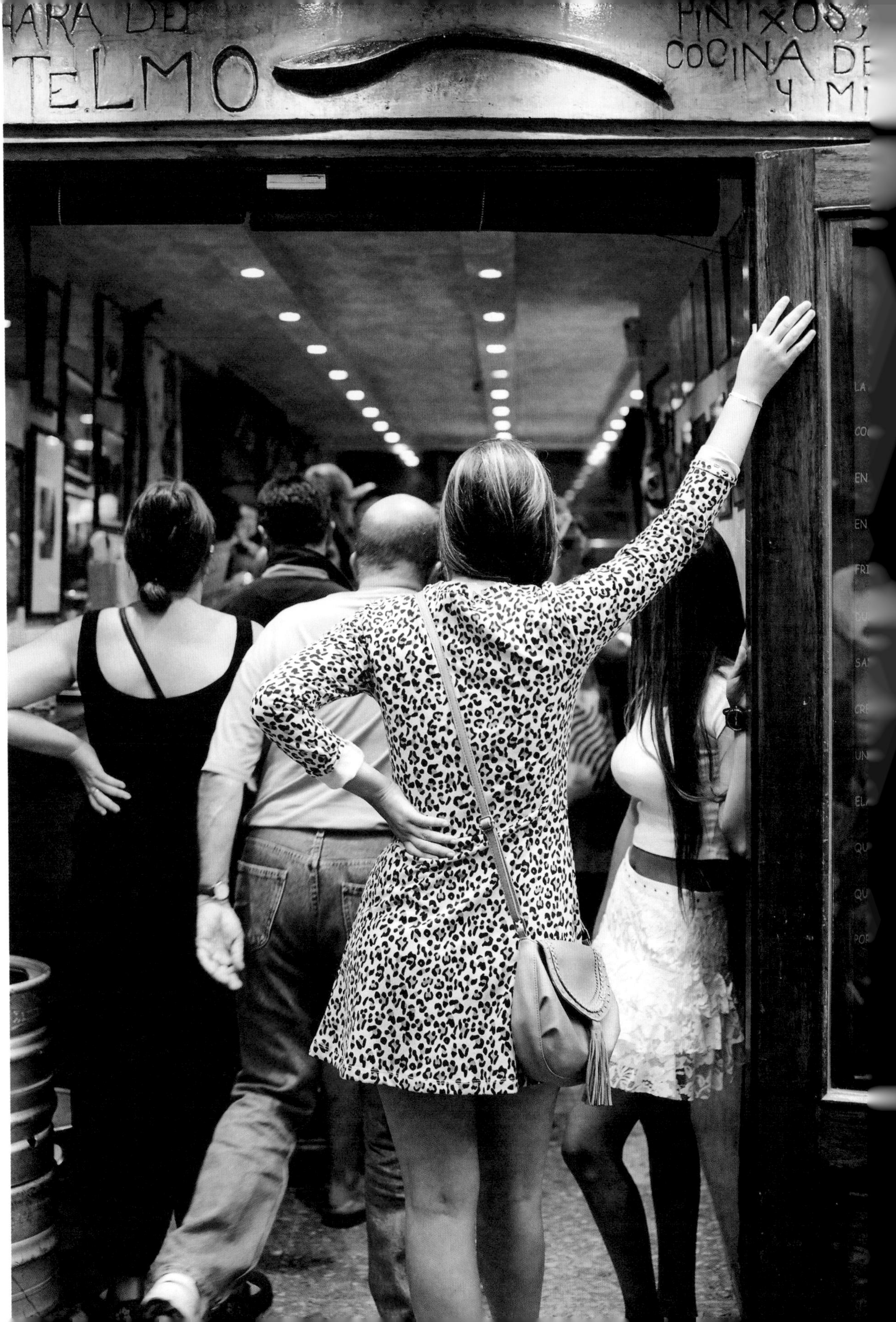
TELMO
PINTXOS,

INTXAURSALTSA

Serves 4

1 litre (34 fl oz) full-fat (whole) milk
1 cinnamon stick
200 g (7 oz) caster (superfine) sugar
250 g (9 oz) walnuts
2 free-range eggs, beaten
plum compote, to serve
    (see page 233)

This is a typical Basque dessert made with walnuts, cinnamon, milk and sugar. It's very easy to make and can be served warm or cold. The name means 'walnut sauce' and in the Basque region it's traditionally served on Christmas Eve.

I like to serve this all year round, particularly when I get the first walnuts of the season from my family's vegetable garden. There's nothing better than fresh walnuts. If you can get hold of them, you should also try making a salad with the Requesón from page 165.

Heat the milk slowly with the cinnamon stick and sugar until the sugar has dissolved and the mixture is almost at boiling point. Remove the cinnamon stick and set aside.

Pound the walnuts in a pestle and mortar until they form a paste. Beat them into the eggs, then gradually stir in the hot milk. Return to the pan and cook over a low heat, stirring constantly, until the mixture thickens to coat the back of a spoon. This will take about 15–20 minutes.

Pour into a dish and leave to cool. Serve with the plum compote, if you like.

CHESTNUT FLAN

Serves 6

700 g (1 lb 9 oz) chestnuts
600 ml (20 fl oz) full-fat (whole) milk
25 g (1 oz) unsalted butter
1 vanilla pod, split and seeds
   scraped
250 g (9 oz) caster (superfine) sugar
2 whole free-range eggs
2 free-range egg yolks

Chestnuts are so popular in the Basque Country as they are found in abundance there. When they are in season, you will see them everywhere, including being roasted in the streets – that smell!

I can't wait for the season to start as they are so versatile for cooking. They make a great addition to stews and salads, and are just wonderful in this flan recipe.

Preheat the oven 220°C (430°F/Gas 7).

Pierce the chestnuts and roast in the oven for 10–15 minutes. Cool and peel. Turn the oven down to 150°C (300°F/Gas 2).

Put the chestnuts in the milk with the butter, vanilla seeds and pod and 100 g (3½ oz) of the sugar. Cook for 20 minutes until the chestnuts are soft. Blend until smooth, then allow to cool a little before beating in the eggs and egg yolks. Set aside.

Put the remaining sugar in a pan and heat very, very gently until the sugar dissolves, swirling the pan to help it caramelise evenly. Once it is a dark amber colour, pour it into the bottom of six 200 ml (7 fl oz) ramekins. Pour the chestnut mixture over the top, then cover each one with foil and place in a roasting tin.

Pour boiling water around the outside of the ramekins so that it comes up about halfway, then bake in the oven for 15 minutes. Remove the foil and bake for a further 10–12 minutes until just set, but with a wobble in the middle.

Allow to cool, then chill until ready to serve. Run a small sharp knife around the outside edge of each ramekin, then turn out onto plates and serve immediately.

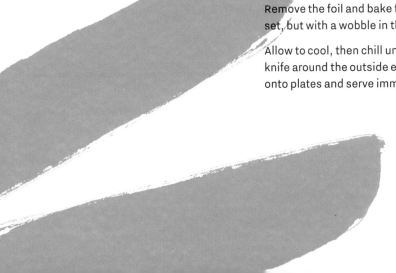

CARAMELISED PEARS WITH HAZELNUT ICE CREAM

Serves 4

25 g (1 oz) unsalted butter
25 g (1 oz) caster (superfine) sugar
4 ripe pears, peeled and cut into
    wedges
1 vanilla pod, split and seeds
    scraped
50 ml (2 fl oz) brandy

for the ice cream
80 g (3 oz) hazelnuts
250 g (9 oz) caster (superfine) sugar
600 ml (20 fl oz) full-fat (whole) milk
6 free-range egg yolks
500 ml (17 fl oz) double (heavy)
    cream

In the middle of October, the first hazelnuts start to appear in the Basque Country. Go and see Lourdes at Ordizia Market, for she is a woman in the know and will always have the first crop on her stall. They make a wonderful garnish for a salad, such as the Requesón on page 165.

Toast the hazelnuts for the ice cream in a pan until lightly golden, then tip onto a baking sheet lined with non-stick silicone or baking paper.

Put 100 g (3½ oz) of the caster sugar in a pan with 1 tablespoon of water, place over a low heat and very gently melt the sugar. Increase the heat and bubble until you have a dark golden caramel. Pour over the hazelnuts and leave to cool. Once cold, bash up into small pieces and set aside.

Heat the milk in a pan to almost boiling. Beat the egg yolks with the remaining sugar until light and fluffy, then pour over the hot milk. Stir until combined, then tip back into a clean pan and cook slowly over a low heat until you have a thick custard. Strain into a bowl and cool. Once cold, add the cream and the hazelnut praline. Pour into an ice-cream maker and churn until set. Scoop into a container and freeze. To make the ice cream by hand, please see the tip on page 209.

Melt the butter and sugar in a pan, add the pears and the vanilla seeds and pod. Cook, turning, for 10–15 minutes until tender and caramelised. Pour in the brandy and bubble until smooth, then divide among bowls or plates and serve with the hazelnut ice cream.

STRAWBERRIES WITH VANILLA OIL & MINT ICE CREAM

When my recipe tester, Lizzie, and I were testing this recipe, we picked the mint from her mum's garden and I have to say that it's some of the best mint I have ever had. It's completely different to the mint we have in Spain, which is much more fragrant. My dad used to bring some home and put it in the kitchen; we could smell it throughout the whole house.

The combination of the subtle mint ice cream and sweet strawberries is just wonderful. I could have a whole pot of this to myself.

Serves 4

200 ml (7 fl oz) very light olive oil
1 vanilla pod
500 g (1 lb 2 oz) ripe strawberries

for the ice cream
600 ml (20 fl oz) full-fat (whole) milk
large bunch of mint, leaves bruised
250 g (9 oz) caster (superfine) sugar
6 free-range egg yolks
500 ml (17 fl oz) double (heavy) cream

To make the ice cream, heat the milk in a pan until almost boiling. Add the bruised mint and set aside to infuse for at least 1 hour, but 2–3 hours is better. Beat the sugar and egg yolks together in a bowl until light and fluffy.

Heat the milk through again, then strain over the egg mixture, stirring until smooth.

Pour back into a clean pan, put over a medium-low heat and cook, stirring constantly, until you have a thick, smooth custard. Pour into a bowl and, when cold, stir in the cream. Pour into an ice-cream maker and churn until set, then scoop into a container and freeze until ready to serve. To make the ice cream by hand, please see the tip on page 209.

Pour the oil into a small pan, halve the vanilla pod and scrape the seeds into the pan, then chop the pod into pieces and add to the pan. Heat very gently for 10–15 minutes, then pour into a sterilised jar and allow to cool and infuse overnight.

When ready to serve, slice the strawberries, drizzle with the vanilla oil and serve with the mint ice cream.

ROAST LAVENDER PEACHES WITH BAKED CUSTARD

Serves 6

600 ml (20 fl oz) full-fat (whole) milk
150 ml (5 fl oz) double (heavy) cream
1 vanilla pod, split and seeds scraped
3 medium free-range eggs
3 free-range egg yolks
185 g (6½ oz) caster (superfine)
    sugar

for the roast lavender peaches
6 peaches
3 tablespoons honey
150 ml (5 fl oz) Patxaran
1 tablespoon lavender seeds

Patxaran is one of my favourite digestifs, so finishing a meal with a glass of this, heaped with ice, is just heaven. The trouble is, one glass is never enough!

This recipe is easy to make and will impress your guests. The aroma of the lavender really complements all of the other flavours in the dish. We are seeing lavender used more and more in cooking, although this is the first time that I have included a recipe using it in my book.

If you can't get Patxaran, some sloe gin will work just as well.

Preheat the oven to 160°C (320°F/Gas 3).

Heat the milk and cream with the vanilla pod and seeds over a low heat until almost boiling.

Whisk the eggs, egg yolks and sugar together, then pour over the hot milk. Mix well, then strain into a 1 litre (34 fl oz) dish. Put the dish in a roasting tin and pour boiling water in around the sides so that it comes about halfway up. Slide into the oven and bake for 35–45 minutes until just set, but with a wobble in the middle. Remove from the oven and set aside to cool.

Increase the oven to 190°C (375°F/Gas 5). Halve the peaches and put in a roasting tin with the honey, Patxaran and lavender. Roast for 30–40 minutes until the peaches are tender. Pour off the juices and reduce to a glossy syrup in a small pan. Serve the roasted peaches with the syrup and baked custard.

PASTEL VASCO

Serves 8

for the jam
200 g (7 oz) cherries, pitted and
    halved
handful of lemon verbena leaves
juice of 1 lemon
90–125 g (3¼–4 oz) jam (jelly) sugar

for the pastry
125 g (4 oz) unsalted butter
100 g (3½ oz) caster (superfine)
    sugar
1 whole free-range egg
1 free-range egg yolk
225 g (8 oz) plain (all-purpose) flour
½ teaspoon baking powder
1 free-range egg, beaten to glaze

for the filling
300 ml (10 fl oz) full-fat (whole) milk
1 vanilla pod, split and seeds scraped
4 free-range egg yolks
50 g (2 oz) caster (superfine) sugar
25 g (1 oz) plain (all-purpose) flour
2 teaspoons cornflour (cornstarch)

Its French name is *gâteau Basque* and in the Basque country it's known as *biskotxa*. It's originally from the Basque region of France, and nowadays it's popular in the Spanish Basque region as well. You can find mentions of this dish as far back as the 17th century, when it was sometimes made with almonds and stuffed with fruit or jam. These days, it's normally made using flour and then filled with crème patisserie. I like it like this, but always add jam too – and why not?

Don't forget to put the *lauburu*, or Basque cross, on top as this is the symbol of the region, and it looks really pretty too.

First, make the jam. Put the cherries in a pan, add the lemon verbena leaves and lemon juice and cook slowly for about 20–25 minutes until the cherries have broken down. Pour into a jug and measure how much juice you have. You want to add about three-quarters of the amount you have in sugar. Tip the fruit and juice back into the pan, add the sugar and gently heat to dissolve the sugar, then bring to the boil. Cook hard until you reach the setting point – this could be as little as 10 minutes. Have a plate in the freezer and when the bubbles start to get slow and sluggish, it is time to test.

Spoon a little of the jam onto the cold plate and push it with your finger. If it wrinkles, then it is ready; if not, then cook for 5 more minutes and test again. Alternatively, you can use a sugar thermometer and take the jam off the heat when the temperature reaches 105°C (221°F). When the jam is ready, pour it into a bowl and set aside to cool completely.

For the pastry, beat the butter and sugar together until really creamy and fluffy. Beat in the egg and egg yolk, then add the flour and baking powder. Bring together to a dough and knead briefly until smooth, then shape into a disc and chill for 30 minutes.

Heat the milk in a pan with the vanilla pod and seeds until almost boiling. Beat the egg yolks and sugar together until fluffy, then add the flours and beat until smooth. Pour over the milk and mix together, then return to the pan over a low heat and cook until you have a very thick, smooth mixture. Spoon into a bowl, cover with cling film (plastic wrap) and leave to cool completely.

Cut off a piece of pastry about 50 g (2 oz) in weight to use to make the *lauburu* (Basque cross). Divide the rest of the pastry into a third and two-thirds. Roll out the bigger bit and use to line the base and sides of a 25 cm (10 in) deep, loose-bottomed cake tin.

Spoon the cold cream filling into the tin, then dot spoonfuls of the jam over the top. Roll out the smaller piece of pastry and cover the jam, trimming away any excess and crimping the sides of the pastry together.

Roll out the last bit of pastry and cut out the Basque cross (you may want to make a template to help you). Brush the top of the pastry with the beaten egg, top with the cross, then glaze again. Chill while you heat the oven to 180°C (350°F/Gas 4).

Bake the pie for 35–45 minutes until golden brown. Leave to cool in the tin before releasing and serving.

CINNAMON FRITTERS WITH PLUM COMPOTE

Serves 6

50 ml (2 fl oz) olive oil
pared zest of 1 orange and 1 lemon
500 g (1 lb 2 oz) plain (all-purpose)
    flour plus extra to dust
1 teaspoon fine sea salt
2 teaspoons dried yeast
75 g (2½ oz) caster (superfine) sugar
4 free-range eggs
50 g (2 oz) unsalted butter, melted
sunflower oil for frying
1 tablespoon caster (superfine)
    sugar mixed with 1 teaspoon
    ground cinnamon to dust

for the compote
700 g (1 lb 9 oz) ripe plums, halved
    and stoned
pared zest of 1 orange
100 g (3½ oz) caster (superfine) sugar
75–100 ml (2½–3½ fl oz) Pedro
    Ximénez

I created this compote recipe to go with my mum's cinnamon fritters, it's the perfect accompaniment. Add an extra of 50 g (2 oz) of caster sugar to the compote if you want a really sweet kick.

Pour the oil into a small pan, add the zests and heat gently for 5 minutes, then set aside to cool and infuse for at least 30 minutes.

Mix the flour, salt, yeast and sugar in a bowl. Make a well in the centre. Strain the infused oil into a jug, mix with the eggs and melted butter, then pour into the dry mixture and stir to mix.

Bring together to a dough with your hands and knead in a stand mixer with a dough hook for 5–10 minutes until smooth and elastic and coming away from the sides. If you don't have a mixer you can use your hands to pull and stretch the dough up and down in a bowl until it stretches up without breaking. Cover the bowl and leave to rise for 2–3 hours (or rise overnight in the fridge).

To make the compote, put the plums and the rest of the ingredients in a pan and heat gently for 10–15 minutes until the plums have started to soften but not broken to mush.

Heat a pan of sunflower oil until it reaches 180°C (350°F).

On a floured surface, roll out the dough as thin as you can and cut into squares about 10–12 cm (4–4½ in) long – you should have about 25 squares.

Fold one corner of a square into the centre, then fold the opposite corner in on top. Dip your finger in water and press the dough where the points meet to seal it together and stop it unrolling.

Fry in batches in the oil for a few minutes until the fritters are golden and puffed. Drain on paper towels and dust straight away with the cinnamon sugar. Serve with the plum compote.

CREAM CHEESE ICE CREAM WITH BLACKCURRANT & CAMOMILE SYRUP

Serves 4–6

for the cheese ice cream
120 g (4 oz) full-fat cream cheese
130 g (4½ oz) Greek yoghurt
100 g (3½ oz) runny honey
20 g (¾ oz) glucose syrup

for the syrup
150 g (5 oz) blackcurrants
100 g (3½ oz) caster (superfine) sugar
generous pinch of dried camomile
    flowers
squeeze of lemon

If you've been lucky enough to go to Elkano in Getaria and try the cheese ice cream, I think it's safe to say that you will never forget it, or anything else that you eat there for that matter. It's one of my favourite restaurants.

I've never asked for the recipe, as apart from anything else, it gives me an excuse to go there! So, this is just my interpretation, but I'm very happy with it. I've added camomile to the syrup as I had some fresh camomile flowers from Ordizia market the last time I went there, and I think it works really well here.

Put the cream cheese, Greek yoghurt, honey and glucose syrup in a pan with 150 ml (5 fl oz) water and gently heat until the cream cheese has melted, whisking to combine. Bring to the boil, cool, then chill for at least 1 hour before churning in an ice-cream maker. Scoop into a plastic container and freeze until needed.

If you don't have an ice-cream maker, pour the mixture into a deep plastic container and freeze for 2 hours, then beat with an electric hand whisk to break up the crystals and freeze for a further hour. Repeat this twice more, then freeze until solid.

Put the blackcurrants in pan with the sugar, camomile and a small splash of water. Bring to the boil, then simmer gently for a couple of minutes until the blackcurrants have all broken down. Pass through a fine sieve back into the pan, then cook gently for 3–5 minutes until you have a glossy drizzling syrup. Add a little lemon juice to taste.

Remove the ice cream from the freezer to soften 15 minutes, then serve a quenelle or scoop of ice cream on a puddle of syrup.

BASQUE MENUS

Don't feel panicked when you think about preparing a pinxtos or multicourse menu. There is so much that you can easily prepare ahead – either in the hours or even days before. This means that on the day of your get-together there will actually be very little to do, and you'll be able to sit down and enjoy your meal with friends and family instead of rushing around.

Pintxos menu 1

For 4

Marinated White Anchovies with Tomatoes & Jamón Salad (page 36)
Pan-Fried Guindiallas (page 155)
Classic Tortilla (page 162)
Russian Salad with Prawns (page 113)

Baked Crab (page 138)
Salad of Partridge Escabeche with Walnuts & Figs (page 32)
Squid Meatballs with Saffron & Almond Sauce (page 128)

Chocolate Pots with Tejas de Tolosa (page 214)

The day before

Make the mayonnaise for the Russian Salad, add the potatoes, carrots, peas and piquillo peppers. Boil the egg. Store in the fridge.

Cook the crabs and pick out all the meat and keep in bowls. Clean the shells. Store in the fridge.

Next, the Partridge Salad. Cook the partridge, shred the meat and toss with the reduced juices. Toast the walnuts. Store in separate airtight containers, and pop the partridge in the fridge.

Make the Squid Meatballs and shape them and chill in the fridge. Make the sauce for the meatballs up until just before you add the saffron and almonds and chill in a bowl. Store in the fridge.

Make the Chocolate Pots and chill. Make the Tejas de Tolosa and keep in an airtight container.

On the day

Toast the baguettes, pile with the Russian Salad and finish with the egg, parsley and prawn.

Make the Tortilla just before people arrive.

Prepare the Marinated White Anchovies salad just before people arrive. Pan-fry the Guindillas

Toss the partridge with the frisee lettuce, add the walnuts and figs.

Warm the sauce for the Squid Meatballs and finish with the saffron and almonds. Fry the meatballs and add to the sauce.

Pintxos menu 2

For 6

Pan-fried Guindillas (or padrón peppers) (page 155)
Toasts with Requesón, Red Peppers & Thyme
  (page 165)
Grilled Green & White Asparagus with Idiazábal
  Smoked Cheese (page 180)

Pintxo of Crab & Prawns (page 131)
Marinated White Anchovies with Tomatoes &
  Jamón Salad (page 36)
Spinach & Goat's Cheese Croquetas (page 150)
Tortilla de Bacalao (page 93)

Pork Trotters, Apple & Hazelnut Terrine (page 24)
Roasted Chicken Wings with Roast Potatoes,
  Parsley & Garlic (page 18)

Pastel Vasco (page 230)

Several days before

Make the Requesón and store in the fridge.

Make the mix for the Croquetas, then make the
Pork Terrine. Store in separate containers in
the fridge.

The day before

Prepare the red peppers for the Toasts and
marinate overnight in the fridge.

Make the pastry and cook the pastry cases for the
Pintxos of Crab & Prawn. Make the mayonnaise and
blend with the crab meat. Store in the fridge.

Shape the Croquetas into balls and store in
the fridge.

Soak the salt cod and store in the fridge.

Marinate the chicken wings andd store in the fridge.

Make the Pastel Vasco.

On the day

Assemble the Toasts.

Fill the Pintxos of Crab & Prawn Pastry cases
shortly before people arrive.

For the salad, add the tomatoes and jamón to the
anchovies with the dressing.

Make the Tortilla de Bacalao a little in advance,
but so it is still warm to serve.

Slice the Terrine ready to sear.

Roast the chicken wings so they are ready just
before people arrive and are hot to serve.

Blanch the asparagus and mix with the oil.

At the last minute

Fry the Guindillas.

Grill the asparagus.

Fry the Croquetas and sear the Terrine.

Simple three course menu

Serves 4–6

Gordal Olives Stuffed with White Anchovies
(page 125)

Tomato Soup with Jamón & Idiazabal (page 48)

Roast John Dory, Alubias de Tolosa & Pancetta
(page 83)

Apple Tatin with Salted Honey Ice Cream
(page 209)

The day before

Roast the tomatoes for the soup. Store in the
fridge.

Make the alubias to go with the John Dory. Store in
the fridge.

Make the Salted Honey Ice Cream and freeze.

Make the caramel and apples for the Tatin. Keep
them in the frying pan, covered with foil.

On the day

Finish making the Tomato Soup a few hours before
people arrive and reheat as people arrive. Top with
the baguette, jamón, cheese and extra thyme just
before serving.

Stuff your Gordal Olives.

Prepare your John Dory and the crispy pancetta
and put the fish and potatoes in to roast just as you
sit down for the nibbles and starter.

Roll out the pastry for the Tatin and cover the
apples. Put in to bake as soon as the fish is out of
the oven.

Feasting menu for friends

Serves 4

Tuna Confit with Guindillas, Anchovy & White
Onion (page 78)

Gambas a la Plancha (page 122)

Tomato Salad with Olive Oil (page 153)

Duck Livers & Chanterelles (page 35)

Chicken Stewed in Cider & Apples (page 55)

Cream Cheese Ice Cream with Blackcurrants &
Camomile Syrup (page 236)

The day before

Confit the tuna. Keep it in its oil in a cool place until
you are ready to serve.

Make the Cream Cheese Ice Cream and freeze.
Make the Camomile Syrup and store in the fridge.

On the day

For the Chicken Stewed in Cider & Apples, brown
the chicken and fry the onion a few hours in
advance. Fry the apple and put the dish in the oven
when your guests arrive. It will rest happily if it is
ready sooner than you are ready to eat it.

Assemble the Tuna Confit pintxos a little ahead of
people arriving.

Prepare the Tomato Salad and leave it to marinate
in the olive oil and salt.

Prepare your prawns for the Gambas la Plancha.
Also, get the Duck Livers & Chanterelles ready for
cooking. These dishes both need to be done at the
last minute, but they are so quick to cook and will
taste much better for being fresh from the pan.

Remove the Cream Cheese Ice Cream from the
freezer 15 minutes before you want to serve it with
the Blackcurrants & Camomile syrup.

Acknowledgements

Thank you to my family. To my sister, Isabel, brother, Antonio, and sister-in-law, Maria José, for being always there, and to my niece and nephews, Carmen, Marina, Cristina, Juan and Antonio, too.

Thanks to the team who worked on the book. Holly Arnold, for making this third one and many more things happen. Demelza Márquez, for making my life easier. Hannah Norris, for all of your help over many years. Lizzie Kamenetzky, for your help with developing the recipes. Laura Edwards, for the wonderful pictures. Kate Pollard, for believing in this project from the start, and for your help all along the way. Emma Marijewycz, Kajal Mistry, Laura Willis and everyone else at Hardie Grant. Clare Skeats, for the amazing design. Jenny Bowers, for the beautiful illustrations.

Thank you to Ken Sanker, for his unconditional support and friendship. Really special thanks to Juan Mari and Elena Arzak for all your support for many years. Enrique Eduardo Ruiz de Lera, Ana Bermúdez and all the team at the STO. Susana Nieto, Iñaki Susperregui and many others for making everything happen for us in San Sebastián. Thanks to Jon Kepa Agirregoikoa, who produces the most amazing goat's cheese.

Thank you to Zoltan Polgar and Victor Calvente and the teams at my restaurants.

Finally, to all my dear chefs for giving me the amazing quotes – I am flattered and honoured.

These are just a few of my favourite restaurants the Basque Country that you must try once in your life:

Akelarre:
Chef Pedro Subijana
(3 Michelin stars)
Paseo Padre Orcolaga, 56,
20008 Donostia, Gipuzkoa

Alameda:
Chef Gorka Txapartegi
(1 Michelin star)
Minasoroeta Kalea, 1,
20280 Hondarribia, Gipuzkoa

Arzak:
Chefs Elena & Juan Mari
(3 Michelin stars)
Avda Alcalde Elósegui, 273,
20015 San Sebastián-Donostia,
Gipuzkoa,

Asador Etxebarri:
Chef Victor Arguinzoniz
(1 Michelin star)
PlazaSan Juán, 1,
48291 Apatamonasterio, Biscay

Azurmendi:
Chef Eneko Atxa (3 Michelin stars)
Legina Auz., s/n, 48195 Larrabetzu,
Bizkaia

Bodegón Alejandro:
Calle de Fermín Calbetón, 4,
20003 Donostia-San Sebastián,
Guipúzcoa

Elkano:
Aitor Arregui (1 Michelin star),
Herrerieta Kalea, 2, 20808 Getaria,
Gipuzkoa

Fuego Negro:
Edorta
Calle 31 de Agosto, 31,
20003 San Sebastián, Gipuzkoa

Gambara:
José, Amaia and Amaiur
General Artetxe Kalea, 8, Donostia,
Gipuzkoa

La bodega Donostiarra:
Chef Mikel
Calle de Peña y Goñi, 13,
20002 Donostia, Gipuzkoa

La Cuchara de San telmo:
Calle del Treinta y Uno de Agosto, 28,
20003 Donostia, Gipuzkoa

Mugaritz:
Chef Andoni Luis Aduriz
(2 Michelin stars)
Aldura Aldea, 20, 20100 Errenteria,
Gipuzkoa

Restaurante Mariñela:
Amaia (1 Michelin star),
Paseo del Muelle, 15,
20003 San Sebastián-Donostia
Gipuzkoa

Sidreria Astarbe:
Kizkitza
Txoritokieta Bidea, 13,
20115 Astigarraga, Gipuzkoa

Vinoteca Bernadina:
Amaia Vitoria-Gasteiz
Kalea, 6, 20018 Donostia, Gipuzkoa

Top, left to right:
Laura Edwards,
Hannah Norris,
Demelza Márquez

Middle, left to right:
Peter Meades,
Kate Pollard,
Lizzie Kamenetkzy

Bottom, left to right:
Holly Arnold,
Clare Skeats

José Pizarro has lived in the UK for 16 years and in that time has worked at some of London's most prestigious Spanish restaurants including Eyre Brothers, Brindisa and Gaudi.

He owns three restaurants in London – José and Pizarro, as well as José Pizarro, which opened its doors in 2015.

In 2014 José was voted one of '100 españoles' – a hugely prestigious award which showcases the top 100 Spaniards around the world, based on how they have brought their talents to the masses and demonstrated their Spanish pride through their work.

INDEX

Basque by José Pizarro

First published in 2016 by Hardie Grant Books

Hardie Grant Books (UK)
5th & 6th Floors
52–54 Southwark Street
London SE1 1UN
www.hardiegrant.co.uk

Hardie Grant Books (Australia)
Ground Floor, Building 1
658 Church Street
Melbourne, VIC 3121
www.hardiegrant.com.au

Text © José Pizarro
Photography © Laura Edwards
Illustrations © Jenny Bowers

British Library Cataloguing-in-Publication Data. A catalogue record
for this book is available from the British Library.

ISBN 978-178488-026-2

Publisher: Kate Pollard
Senior Editor: Kajal Mistry
Editorial assistant: Hannah Roberts
Design and Art Direction: Clare Skeats
Photography: © Laura Edwards
Illustrations: © Jenny Bowers
Home Economist: Lizzie Kamenetkzy
Prop Stylist: Polly Webb-Wilson
Copy Editor: Kay Delves
Proofreader: Lorraine Jerram
Indexer: Cathy Heath
Colour Reproduction by p2d

Printed and bound in China by 1010

10 9 8 7 6 5 4 3 2 1

**A note on oven temperatures: If you are using a fan-assisted
oven, please reduce the oven temperatures in the recipes by
20°C (36°F/1 or 2 Gas marks).**